C BOY

DR. FRANK E. GODFREY, SR.

outskirts
press

Outskirts Press, Inc.
http://www.outskirtspress.com

ISBN: 978-1-4787-6259-1

Outskirts Press and the "OP" logo are trademarks belonging to Outskirts Press, Inc.

PRINTED IN THE UNITED STATES OF AMERICA

Table of Contents

CHAPTER 1

It was a nice, cool, summer evening in the Port City in 1945. A full moon reflected off the lake while the chirps from the crickets and other bugs echoed from the underbrush of the giant oak trees that lined the streets. A gentle breeze full with the fragrant smell of the Ashley River gently caressed my face.

Mama would usually dress me real comfortably and take me for a nice ride in my Cadillac-like carriage just about every night. It sat on four springs—it was real nice and comfortable. It was made of real leather, too! They don't make them like that anymore. Mama would usually push me for several blocks to make me sleepy and ready for bed.

We had just about completed our walk around the lake and we were heading back home beside the "colored" Roper Hospital. You see, there were two Roper Hospitals—one for the whites and one for the blacks. I and my three brothers, as well as most other black folks in Charleston, were born at the Colored Roper. That was just the way it was in The South.

We had just passed the hospital when these two

older white ladies approached us. They looked down curiously at me in the carriage. "Oh, that is a fine looking child. Whose baby are you taking care of Annie?"

Most white people called most black women Annie and called most black men Tom. This was just the way it was in Charleston and I guess it was the same way in most of the South; at least it seemed that way.

"This is my child," Mama replied.

"Don't get smart with me, Annie! How can that be your baby? Now who's baby is it?"

You see, I was what you might call a "throwback." I had very light skin, blonde hair, and would eventually have freckles. I would have the blonde hair and freckles until I was ten! Mama's skin was cherry brown and she had straight black hair and high cheekbones. Her mother was from West Africa and had dark skin, kinky hair, a wide nose, and full lips. No one knew where her father was from.

Mama, like most of the women in those days, chose to stay home and raise her children until they were old enough to go to school. She, along with some of her friends, worked at the American Tobacco factory on the other side of town. Charleston was literally divided into two halves by King Street. Anyone living on either side lived "across town." It was almost like two cities and anyone from either side was not safe "across town." I remember Mama coming home most times smelling like fresh tobacco. She also crocheted and sold her work in the neighborhood.

She was a proud woman. Mama never finished high school and it's no telling what she might have become if she had the opportunity to get an education. She could read and took care of all of the family's finances. She was also an excellent, self-taught, piano player and sung in the Adult Choir at Emanuel AME Church on Calhoun Street, which was one of the stops on the underground railroad. Mother Emanuel was a beautiful, white stone church, with her proud steeple and green metal roof protruding majestically towards the heavens. It was just two blocks from the huge bronze statue of the staunch racist, John C. Calhoun.

My father was light-skinned, with somewhat straight hair. Daddy's father was of African and Native American descent and his mother was of African and European descent. His mother, Georgianna Hayes, died during a hurricane. I never knew her and no one ever talked about her either.

Daddy worked at the Naval Shipyard, as many of the black men did. It was considered to be one of the "good" jobs. He also did numerous odd jobs on weekends such as detailing cars, yard work, painting houses, custodial work, waiting tables, and bartending at social functions for white folks—mainly for the naval officers who were based at the shipyard. He often worked on New Year's Eve. He would call us from wherever he was, but I can't remember him ever being with us to welcome in the New Year. He always worked during the Army/Navy Football game. The naval officers would have a big party at the Officer's Club. It started about two hours before kick-off and lasted long after the final whistle blew. I still do not like to watch Army and Navy play.

Daddy always dressed like he was going to church when he went out on the weekends—suit, tie, nice shirt, shoes shined and a Dobson or Hobbs hat. Most men wore dress hats. Daddy probably had about five, each a different color.

He worked real hard to make sure that we had a relatively good life. He never finished high school either. He dropped out of school and worked to help his older sister go to college and she would eventually look down on him with scorn since he wasn't "educated." He was a proud man, but it was hard being black in Charleston, and even harder being a black man.

Daddy had to be at work at 7 o'clock so he would leave each morning before we were out of bed. They were carpooling way back then. Daddy and three of his friends would drive to work together. Each would drive one week of each month. Each morning, just before he left for work, Daddy would always pull our shirts back and blow real hard on our stomachs, making a sound like someone was breaking wind. We would giggle. That was fun and we looked forward to it. We would not see him again until around six o'clock in the evening. I looked forward to his coming home and sometimes I would meet him on the corner and ask him for a nickel to buy a candy bar or some ice cream. You could get a lot for a nickel back then.

Apparently, my color and hair was passed on to

me from my European ancestry, which was two generations back on my father's side. And, to make it worse, my three brothers were all dark.

"This is my baby," Mama said again, almost yelling.

"There is no way that that can be your baby. And, when I find out who you are working for, I'm gonna make it hard for you. You just wait and see. You are a smart mouth girl, ain't you? Go on and get out of my sight! Your baby? You have got to be out of your mind!"

Mama, almost running, pushed my stroller as fast as she could, trying to distance herself from these ignorant and evil women. Tears trickled down her face all the way home and she was sobbing when she entered our home on 71 Kracke Street. Kracke Street was just two blocks long. It began at Spring Street. We lived on the un-paved, dead-end side just across Bogard Street. It would be called a cul-de-sac today. Kennedy Street bordered us in the rear.

The Godfrey Home, 71 Kracke Street Circa 1963

Mama was still sobbing when we got inside. "What's wrong, Tavie?" my father asked. My mama's real name was Octavia, but most people called her Tavie for short. Some of her closest friends also called her Tonki, but I never knew why.

Mama related the story to daddy, sobbing even harder.

"Bill, why are white folks so evil? This is my baby, but they just wouldn't believe me when I told them so. I ain't gonna walk Frank around there no more. They said that they were gonna make trouble for me."

"It's gonna be alright," Daddy said. He pulled Mama into his arms and gently embraced her, and patted her on her back trying to comfort her as she continued to sob.

Mama eventually composed herself. She bathed me in the bathroom sink and pampered me with Johnson's baby oil and baby powder. She dressed me in my little pajamas, gave me a big hug, then kissed me on the cheek and tucked me in.

"Good night, my child," Mama whispered.

Mama knew what I would go through because of my light skin and my blonde hair. She, too, had endured some of the same frustrations growing up. The other children would always tease her and call her names. They would chase her home just about every day. She had straight black hair, but at least she had nice brown skin. The incident with the two white ladies would be small compared to the taunting I would endure from my own people for the rest of my life.

It was gonna be tough enough being black in this

racist town. Everything in Charleston was segregated, from the churches to the schools. Blacks lived in their own neighborhoods, and whites lived in theirs. However, I would learn that my greatest pain would be inflicted by my own people. I would be despised by white folks for being black; despised by most other light-skinned blacks because I didn't think and behave like they did; and I would also be despised by dark-skinned blacks for not being "black enough."

CHAPTER 2

We lived on the top floor of a white, neatly-painted, two-story wood-frame house with dark green shutters. The section of the street on which we lived was referred to as Kracke Court. The street was paved between Spring and Bogard Streets, but the section on which we lived was unpaved. The dirt was more like beach sand. Every time it rained, huge puddles of water would form at the entrance to the street.

Our house was what would be called a shotgun house—if you shot a bullet through the front door, it would go through every room in the house.

A dark green picket fence that daddy had built and painted, stretched across the front yard. Most of the houses in our neighborhood had wooden picket fences.

Two large gates that swung open allowed access to the side yard to the left of the house, where daddy would sometimes park his car. We always had a car. Daddy and Mama didn't like to ride the city bus because black folks had to sit in the back of the bus. A huge sign was posted at the front of the bus warning that all colored passengers must sit behind the white line. A thick, white line was painted in the middle of the bus by the exit door. Black folks had to stand up if there were no colored seats left, even if there were seats in front of the bus. Daddy bought his first car for ninety dollars and financed it for twelve months!

A small gate allowed access to the steps that led to the downstairs porch. The front yard was very small and had neatly trimmed wax-leaf Ligustrum hedges. There were small hedges just in front of the two downstairs windows. There was just enough room in the front yard to allow for the trimming of the hedges.

Four concrete steps led to the downstairs porch that ran almost the length of the house and allowed access to the wooden steps midway on the left that led upstairs. Mama kept a lot of plants on the upstairs porch and on the windowsills. Window plants were the original burglar alarms, as anyone who tried to break into a house through a window would inevitably knock over some plants and the noise would warn anyone inside of an intruder, and might even alert some of the neighbors.

Our parents' bedroom faced the street. Their bedroom had a dresser, a double bed and a rocking chair that was usually covered with the clothes my parents had worn for the week. There was also a staircase that led to the front room downstairs, but the room was closed off as Miss Hattie White lived there.

The living room, where my brothers and I slept,

had a couch, a bunk bed and a double bed. There was also a door that opened to the porch. An old Dumont television sat in the corner of the living room along with an old fan that was held together with lots of black electrical tape. The fan circulated the hot air in the room and sat next to the television on a small wooden table. One summer the old fan got so hot from working so hard and so long that it just went up in flames! That scared us a bit.

Just beyond the living room was the dining room, although we only ate in it on Thanksgiving and Christmas. It had a nice, huge bureau, a china cabinet which held our "good" china, and silverware and a matching table that we used to do our homework. A huge oil stove sat against the back wall. Mama's sewing machine was also in there. Just about everyone had a sewing machine in those days. Primarily, the dining room was used as a passageway to and from the kitchen and as access from the porch.

The kitchen was very small and cluttered. It was probably about 8 feet by 10 feet. It housed a refrigerator, a small table that could seat two, and a wringer washing machine. The machine had no spin cycle, so the wet clothes had to be hand-fed through these two hand-cranked rollers seated just on top of the washing machine to wring out as much water as possible. The rollers looked just like the rolling pins used to roll out dough. After wringing, the clothes would be hung on the clothesline that ran the length of the upstairs porch. There was also a four-burner gas stove and a small sink. Used paper grocery bags were stacked behind the kitchen door. Those were the original trash bags.

Just off the kitchen was an extremely small bathroom that I literally hated to use. Although it was clean, it was very small with no space between the tub, sink, and toilet, and most of the fixtures were rusted. They were probably installed when the old house was built decades earlier. Since bathing was such a chore, we usually took bird baths—where you would just fill the sink with water and use a washcloth to get your body clean.

We did not have a hot water heater so when we took a bath we had to heat up some water on the stove in huge pots. This would take a long time. We were always clean though. Baths were usually reserved for the weekends. Showers did not exist.

We had lots of roaches—the large, flying kinds that some people called water bugs. It wasn't because our house wasn't clean; it's just the way it was in Charleston. The weather was hot and humid, the way the roaches loved it! They usually came out at night. Sometimes, when you went into the kitchen and turned the light on, you could see them scurrying back to their hiding places. Daddy would always get upset as it seemed that every time someone came to visit us, one of the huge roaches would race across the floor or fly across the room.

You could walk down most streets at night, and see huge roaches crawling everywhere and feel and hear them being crushed under your feet. I hated roaches and still do. My children do, too, especially my daughter, Shannon.

Daddy hated roaches, too. On the other hand, it was more like a phobia. If Daddy saw a roach in a room, he couldn't rest until he had killed it. His father was the same way. Daddy once told us that his father shot a huge hole through the roof of the house where he was born in Summerville, South Carolina with a shotgun, trying to kill a roach. Daddy always kept one of those manual insecticide spray cans nearby to fight the roaches. You would fill the container with the pesticide and push this long handle to dispense the spray. The most effective spray we used was called "Real Kill." Fighting roaches was a constant battle.

I will never forget one night when it was so hot that my T-shirt clung to my sweating flesh. In the middle of the night, I felt something trying to work its way up my back. It was scratching and biting. At first I thought that I was dreaming until I realized that a huge roach was crawling up my back! I reached up under my shirt, grabbed it and squeezed it as hard as I could. Some of its guts were all over my hand. I threw it on the floor besides the bed. I don't know if I ever got back to sleep. The next morning there was little left of the roach as the soldier ants had carried most of it away and they were still working on the rest.

Mama gave birth to four sons: Buck, Bobby, John and me. Buck was the first-born and I was second, born eighteen months after Buck. I was followed by Bobby five years later, and John ten years later. Buck and I shared the double bed in the living room that had a stagecoach etched in the middle of the head-board, marking the two sides of the bed. We were both careful not to cross the stagecoach. My two younger brothers, Bobby and John, shared the bunk bed. Bobby slept on the top bunk and John took the bottom.

I also had another brother, Rodney, who was still-born. He would have been right after Bobby. Our parents wanted four children, preferably boys, as my father was the last male in the family. He wanted sons to carry on the family's name.

A white man named Mr. Padgett, who was my father's supervisor at the Shipyard, always had some odd jobs on the weekends for Daddy to do. One day, he gave my father a grown, little black and white bulldog named Butch. Mama was about seven months pregnant with Rodney.

One day, Butch got out of the yard and my mother chased him for several blocks before she finally caught him. She was exhausted and was holding her stomach when she returned home. I don't know if she chased him because she feared that my father would be angry or because she didn't want the white folks to think that we were irresponsible. I doubt that she cared too much for the dog.

Anyway, when Mama went to the hospital to deliver Rodney, I remember Buck, Bobby, and I sitting by the telephone, eagerly waiting for the call from my father who was at the hospital, to tell us if we had a little brother or a little sister. I still remember being told that our little brother was born dead. Chasing Butch had been just too much for Mama and Rodney I guess. I never really cared too much for Butch in the first place, and liked him less after that.

My grandfather, Joshua Eden Godfrey, owned the house at 71 Kracke Street and he and my step-grandmother, Mary Ellen Huger (pronounced Hugee), lived on the bottom floor. I never had much to do with my grandfather. In fact, I never saw him that much. It seemed like the shades in the windows in his part of the house were always closed and it was always dark inside.

I only remember him as being mean. I never had a good feeling when I was around him and can't remember him ever saying anything nice. I never remember sitting on his lap or even having a conversation with him. He had cherry-colored skin and straight black hair. He used to be a butcher. He knew a great deal about animals. My cousin said that he had a degree in Veterinary Science, but was not allowed to practice in Charleston. She also said that this contributed to his anger. I always thought that he was a self-taught veterinarian. It was obvious that he was a smart man.

After he died Buck and I found several vials of worms he had taken from the stool of various dogs and other animals that he had preserved and labeled for identification and treatment.

Grandpa Josh had two, mean German Shepherds—Jack and Jill. They were so mean that my brothers and I couldn't even play in our own yard. They were just like my grandfather. One day, the police had to come to the house and shoot both of them dead. I wasn't saddened by their deaths. When my grandfather died, I don't remember being sad either. I don't even remember his funeral.

My grandparents rented the downstairs front room and the back room to two, nice, old black ladies for about ten dollars a month. Miss Hattie White lived in the twenty by twenty foot front room, just below my parents, bedroom, and Miss Rosa Johnson lived in the small back room, which was about fourteen by fourteen feet.

Miss Rosa and Miss Hattie worked for some white folks, cooking and cleaning and doing whatever else the white folks wanted. They were called domestics. I never saw much of them on weekdays, as they left home before the crack of dawn to prepare the white folks breakfast. Night would fall before their return as they also had to prepare dinner and wash the dishes before they could leave. Their white bosses were much younger than Miss Rosa and Miss Hattie but they still called them by their first names. However, Miss Rosa and Miss Hattie had to call their bosses Mr. and Mrs.

Miss Rosa had a slight hump on the right side of her back, walked sort of bent over, and used a walking cane. She would sometimes sadly relate to me how some of the ignorant children would tease her by calling her a hag when she passed them on her way home from the bus stop each day. I could see the immense pain on her face and it really hurt me, too. Those children didn't know Miss Rosa, for if they had really known her, they would never have treated her like that. Sometimes, she would carry candy with her to offer to the children to prove to them that she was a nice lady. However, the kids would never come close enough to her to really find out how nice she was.

One day, I met Miss Rosa at the bus stop and held her hand as we walked pass those children and to show them that she was nice. I looked them right in their eyes as we walked pass. This time, the children didn't tease her and Miss Rosa said that they never teased her again. That made me feel very happy, and I know it made Miss Rosa happy, too.

The only window in Miss Rosa's small room faced the backyard. She had a small bed, which was just large enough for one person that sat against a wall. A single-burner oil stove sat in the middle of the room and provided heat, and a place to cook. A small wooden table with two folding chairs sat next to the stove. A metal pan sat on the table and was used to retrieve water to wash off just as some cowboys did in old

Westerns. A single spigot sink provided a place to wash her dishes. A small dresser and an icebox completed the room. Miss Rosa's little room was always neat.

Everyone had an icebox, which was a thick wooden box with one or two doors. A block of ice would be placed in the ice box and covered with newspaper to keep it from melting too quickly. Food would be packed around the ice to keep it cold.

The iceman would make daily trips to the neighborhood each morning around 9 or 10 and each afternoon around 2 or 3. You could buy a small block of ice for 12 cents and a large block for 25 cents. The iceman used to always chip us off a piece of that good, cold ice for us to cool us off. The visits from the iceman were a fun part of the day for everyone.

There was also an ice house around the corner on Spring Street near Rutledge Avenue and people who missed the iceman could be seen walking home with a block of ice held by a piece of twine. On a real, hot day, you could follow the drips from the melting ice down the street. Depending on how far one lived from the ice house as much as half of the ice might be melted by the time the person got home. A 25-cent block might only be worth 12 cents by the time one made it home from the ice house.

Miss Rosa shared a common bathroom with a tub with Miss Hattie on the bottom floor. I spent many hours with Miss Rosa, talking and eating wheat bread topped with butter and brown sugar. She always had that for me. It was one of our rituals.

She would always come upstairs to visit us on Christmas Eve and bring each of us a little gift to put under the Christmas tree. She didn't come upstairs otherwise as those nineteen steps were too hard on her fragile legs and feet. Her feet were crooked and she had the biggest bunions I have ever seen! We would always go and visit her in her little room.

One day, Miss Rosa got sick and her family took her away to live with her daughter across town. I had never really seen much of her family as they seldom came by to visit Miss Rosa. Miss Rosa couldn't work anymore. I never saw her after they took her away. I heard that she had grown sicker and they put her in the hospital where she died. I never saw my friend again. I learned of her death long after she had been buried. I had lost someone whom I loved very much, and never got the chance to go to her funeral or even say goodbye. I still think of Miss Rosa very often.

Miss Hattie's room was much larger than Miss Rosa's. She had a bigger bed and some furniture in her room and a two-burner oil stove. She also had a larger icebox than Miss Rosa. Miss Hattie smoked a lot of cigarettes and her room always smelled like old tobacco and her teeth were brown from tobacco stains. She was a real nice lady, too. She walked erect and never had to deal with what Miss Rosa had to deal with—nobody teased her and called her names.

I knew Miss Hattie for most of my young life. When the interstate highway came through in 1963 and our home was demolished, we moved to the other end of Kracke Street near Spring Street and Miss Hattie moved to the country to a place called John's Island. I would still visit her with my parents, but it was not like having her right downstairs. I promised Miss Hattie, when I was very young, that I would buy her a house one day, but she died before I could fulfill my promise. Miss Hattie and Miss Rosa were two of the nicest people I have ever known other than my parents, my grandmother, Mary Ellen, and my Aunt Lillie.

Aunt Lillie was my Grandmother Smalls' sister. She lived on the land handed down to our family by her father, a newly-freed slave named Samson Duckson. She was one of the nicest persons I knew. She usually had a corn pipe in her mouth, similar to what Popeye smoked, although most of the time it wasn't lit. Aunt Lillie smoked tobacco and her front teeth were stained dark brown from the smoke.

I always looked forward to seeing my Aunt Lillie. Then one day Aunt Lillie got sick and they wouldn't allow her to stay in the hospital because she hadn't paid into Social Security. "They done sent me home to die, Frankie," Aunt Lillie shared with me. I felt so helpless. How could anyone treat someone like that? Especially my Aunt Lillie.

Aunt Lillie farmed the land her father left her and she sold her produce in the City Market near downtown Charleston every Friday and Saturday. She would transport her crops on a wooden, horse-drawn wagon. The trip to Charleston took at least an hour. She would arrive around 7:00 and would stay until almost dark or until she had sold all of her crops. We would take Aunt Lillie some breakfast that Mama had cooked and hang out with her and some of the other family who might have come with her. That was so much fun!

Aunt Lillie only lived for a few months after she was sent home to die. When she died it seemed like a piece of me went with her. I still think about her with feelings of joy mixed with sadness.

Shortly after the death of my grandparents, my parents rented the space between where Miss Rosa and Miss Hattie lived to the MacBeths. Mr. MacBeth was a semi-retired mechanic and Mrs. MacBeth worked as a housekeeper for some white folks. The Macbeths were also very nice, but I seldom saw much of them. Mr. MacBeth liked to sit around with the other retired men under the pecan tree across from our house and play checkers and tell jokes. You would usually only see Mrs. MacBeth when she was going to and from work.

Mrs. MacBeth died from a heart attack she suffered when trying to run to catch the bus that would take her to work. People said that the white bus driver saw her running to catch the bus, but he sped off anyway. She was trying to get to the white folks house on time, but she never made it. I could never understand how that driver could do that. I guess he was about as ignorant as the kids who called my friend Miss Rosa a hag. Mr. MacBeth later died from sugar diabetes.

Many of the women in my little neighborhood worked as domestics. Most of them would leave their own children to the care of the neighborhood and the streets while they took care of the white folks' children. That worked okay, however, as everyone in the neighborhood looked out for each other.

My step-grandmother, Mary Ellen Huger, was one of the nicest persons I have ever known, although my brother, Buck, did not care for her too much. He said that she was mean to him. It may well have been that Buck was dark-skinned and I was light-skinned. However, I never witnessed any of that and to me she was nice.

To be honest, I could not understand how she had ever married my grandfather. They were so different. I spent much of my free time with her. She would walk me to school each day and would be there when I got out of school. We would always stop by this little corner grocery store across from Immaculate Conception School (ICS) on the corner of Coming Street and Cannon Street. She would buy me an ice cream of my choice—usually an ice cream sandwich. I would enjoy my ice cream as I held her gentle and comforting hand all the way home. I looked forward to those days.

When we got home, she would often sit in this

huge rocking chair on the downstairs porch with me nestled on her lap and gently rock back and forth as she either read or sang to me or maybe we would just talk. She would always fix me some wheat bread with butter and sugar on it just like Miss Rosa did. It was so good!

Once, as she was rocking me, one of the huge ornamental shutters got caught under the top of the rocking chair and unhinged, striking me right on the top left side of my head. I still have the scar today. Grandma was very sad. She thought that she had seriously injured me. It was very painful. I ran upstairs to my mother and she held me and cleaned up the wound. I would have a slight headache for a couple of days, but I was all right. Grandma never rocked me in that chair again and it didn't bother me a bit.

One day, as my grandmother was going to meet the mailman, she slipped on the front steps, fell, and broke her hip and they had to put her in the hospital. While in the hospital, she contracted pneumonia and died. The next time I saw her she was in a coffin. I remember my father taking me to see her at Mazyck's Funeral Home. I spoke to her but she didn't answer. She didn't even look at me. I gently touched her cheek and it was puffy and cold, not soft and warm as it was when she used to give me those warm hugs. I told my father that it felt like they had packed her cheeks with paper. That was the first time I had ever seen a dead person, and it was my best friend.

Mr. Walter Mazyck owned and operated the funeral home. He had very fair skin and real straight hair. He looked whiter than I did. He learned his profession at a white mortuary school. They didn't admit blacks, but he applied anyway. In those days, most colleges, universities and professional schools, including many of the so-called Negro colleges and universities, required you to send a recent photo with your application.

Many of the black colleges discriminated based on skin color. If you were light-skinned, you had a better chance of being admitted. If you were dark-skinned, you had a tougher time unless your parents were doctors, lawyers, teachers or some other professional.

Since Mr. Mazyck looked white, they admitted him. They never knew that he was a black man. He would joke about that all the time.

His funeral parlor was right around the corner from our house on Ashley Avenue between Spring Street and Bogard Street. It looked just like a house. He and his wife lived on the top floor and the embalming rooms and funeral parlor were on the first floor. You could walk pass his house and see several bodies on display for viewing through the front windows. The rooms were always lighted with dim red lights. We did not like walking pass his house and usually walked on the other side of the street.

Mr. Mazyck was a nice man. My father worked for him for a while, picking up dead bodies. We also kept his vehicles looking good. My father, my brothers, and

I washed and waxed cars on most weekends to bring in extra money. They call it detailing today. We might get about five dollars for a car and maybe ten dollars for a hearse. I hated cleaning Mr. Mazyck' hearses though; not just because they were so big, but because of what they were used for. We also painted houses, did yard work and cleaned a few buildings. My brothers and I never got any of the money—it all went into the household.

Since my grandmother and I were so close, the old folks used to wonder whether she would come back to take me to heaven with her. There was this myth that when two people were as close as my grandmother and I were when one died, the other would come back and "get them." I used to hear my mother's friends talk about it all of the time, but it didn't scare me. I really missed my best friend and maybe I wanted her to come and get me so that I could be with her. Ever since that happened I seemed to have this fear of losing anyone that I had grown close to.

After my grandmother's death, I would peek into my parents' bedroom each night to make sure that they were breathing before I would go to sleep. I had lost Miss Rosa and my grandmother and could not think of losing either of my parents. I knew that they would pass on one day, but I hoped that it would happen when I was grown up so I might be able to better handle it—or so I thought.

Shortly after my grandfather died, we took over

the whole house. For some reason, my Aunt Ocala seemed to want Daddy to buy her share of the house before we could take over the rest of the house. This upset Daddy a lot. I couldn't understand it then and it would take years before I knew the truth. It seems that my aunt never felt that my mother was worthy of "being in the family." Several years later, when my Aunt Ocala was near death I would learn the truth.

My cousin Ruth, the daughter of my father's brother (Joshua Godfrey, Jr.), called me to ask me if I could meet her in Charlotte. I had never met Joshua, but I heard that he was mean just like his father, whom he was named for. My father told me that Josh Sr. and Josh Jr. did not get along.

My father told us that one time Josh Jr. wanted to go hunting and my grandfather told him that he couldn't go and he decided to go anyway. Just as he was rushing to leave through the front gate, the gate swung closed and the gun went off, blowing off his right arm. He eventually moved to New York where he met and married Ruth's mother. Ruth said that she heard that he had lost his arm in a hunting accident.

CHAPTER 3

My Aunt Ocala wanted us to come to Charlotte, North Carolina because her husband, Uncle Edward (William Edward Bluford), had recently had a stroke. He was 92 years old and Aunt Ocala was 89. Aunt Ocala was still recovering from being very ill. She lost 40 pounds and looked like she weighed no more than 75 lbs.

They both felt that they were near death and wanted to make sure that their estate was properly administered. They wanted Ruth and me to be co-executors. I agreed, but I didn't know why—maybe it was because of Ruth. Ruth was 68 years old, but didn't look a day over 50. I hadn't seen Ruth for over 40 years! There was a serious split in the family many years ago and we never really got to know each other. When my daughter, Shannon, moved to New York, I began to know and to love Ruth. I regret that we had lost 40 years!

Aunt Ocala and Uncle Edward were unable to have children so they adopted a baby boy and named him William. William was now in his early forties. He had been married several times and had several children. Two of the children lived with Aunt Ocala and Uncle Edward. The boy who stayed there was 22 and unemployed and the girl, who also had a child of her own, was 20. She worked at a fast food restaurant. They had literally killed Uncle Edward and Aunt Ocala. It seems that they had aged so much over the past few years.

I arrived at the hospital where Uncle Edward was being treated. Every patient in the hospital was recovering from a serious illness, most of them rehabilitating from strokes. It was quite depressing. Aunt Ocala and Ruth were nowhere to be found and the nurses pointed me to an exercise room where I could find Uncle Edward.

There he was, strapped in a wheelchair that was more like a large baby walker. I had always been so impressed with how well Uncle Edward had aged, and now he looked older than his 92 years. He seemed to recognize me, but only briefly, as he began to mumble sentences that made little or no sense. I tried to communicate with him to no avail. He had some beans on the front of his shirt that he had apparently either thrown up or failed to get into his mouth. His therapist came in to take him to another room and he tried to resist. I gave him a hug and she wheeled him away.

The nurse told me that I could find Ruth and Aunt Ocala in the cafeteria. I hadn't seen Aunt Ocala since my son Marlin's graduation from North Carolina A&T

about four years earlier. When I approached them, I couldn't believe how Aunt Ocala looked. She looked like a skeleton covered with too much skin for her frame. I tried not to show my surprise at how she looked.

Ocala was almost too weak to bite through her ham and turkey sandwich. It reminded me of how weak my father was just a few hours before he died in 1991. They looked almost like twins and I could see my father through her strained veil. She talked about how her grandchildren were so much trouble for her and Uncle Edward.

"Grands," she yelled with a sigh.

I remember Uncle Edward pulling me to the side at my son's college graduation, telling me, "Frank, these children are literally killing me and your aunt. They are so much trouble."

They had none of the Godfrey blood flowing through their veins. I would later learn that Aunt Ocala and Uncle Edward planned to leave their entire estate to their adopted son and the two grandchildren that stayed with them.

After they finished eating we went back up to see Uncle Edward. There he was in his walker with his head leaning to one side as if it was too heavy for him to hold upright. The nurses had put him in front of the wrong room, but it was right next to his room. He seemed irritated and began to attempt to roll himself into his room. The brake was on and this only added to his frustration. I don't think that he wanted us to see him like this. I freed the brake and pushed him into the room.

He turned the wheelchair facing his bed and acted like he wanted to stand up and lay on the bed, but he was strapped in. He began to talk as if he was in New York. Since Ruth lived in New York, he apparently thought that he was in New York.

It really hurt to see this man, whom I had always admired for his brilliance, intelligence, and manly stature, barely able to articulate a simple sentence. He was a professor at Johnson C. Smith University in Charlotte, North Carolina for decades and served on the board of trustees at the University of North Carolina at Charlotte.

I remember his telling us about the time he had his car stolen with all of the research materials he had spent five years collecting for his dissertation lying on the back seat. The car was recovered, but his research was never found. As a result, he never earned his PhD, but I always looked to him as having earned it. It took a strong individual to accept that reality, but he was a strong man. He always wore some nice, neatly creased pants, held in place with some stylish suspenders, a neatly ironed shirt, and he always sported a bow tie. He also sported a gray mustache similar to Hitler's.

We finally said our goodbyes to Uncle Edward. He said that he would drive us home. He didn't realize that he was in a hospital and couldn't leave. I hugged him, realizing that this might well be the last time I would see him alive. I had grown to accept death and to recognize its early stages.

We left the hospital in time to meet the attorney to discuss the will and to make Ruth and me executors. During the meeting it was disclosed that the estate might well be valued at more than 500,000 dollars and all of the money would go to the children. Aunt Ocala and Uncle Edward had five nieces and nephews and numerous grand nieces and nephews by blood, but none of them were included in the will.

Ruth had told me weeks earlier that Ocala had not included me or any of my brothers in the will because we "never called her." Ruth was right. We did talk, however. We would see them at graduations, weddings, and funerals. I would try to visit them each time I went to Charlotte, and had stayed with them several times, but there was a big void in our relationship.

My father would get upset each time he would learn that Ocala might be in town and might stop by. You could see the veins on the side of his head swelling. She would sometimes come to Charleston and not even come by to see us. We would learn that she was in town from some of the neighbors who might see her. She would be within five minutes of our house and wouldn't come by! I saw her one time while she was visiting her friends, but she didn't see me. Daddy often reminded us of how he had dropped out of school to help her go to college and she looked down on him for not finishing high school. I had always tried not to let the way I really felt about her show, but it was very hard showing her any affection, knowing how she had treated my father and her brother. I just couldn't understand how that could happen.

While at the lawyer's office, Ocala spent more time talking about how I had finished Harvard and was now a college professor, how Ruth's son had graduated from Rutgers and was now working in a New York bank, and how my son Frank had a degree in Geology. Ocala had always placed a great deal of value on credentials and it was sickening to hear her rant and rave to this white female lawyer who I was sure could care less about what was happening in any of our lives.

We finally finished at the lawyer's office and now we had to go back to the hospital to pick up Ocala's car. She hadn't driven it for almost ten years, as Uncle Edward did all of the driving. I took them to the car and followed them back to Ocala's house, not knowing what we would find when we got there.

Following Aunt Ocala to her house was one challenge. She was creeping along at about 20 miles per hour. At least twice, she suddenly appeared to remember that she needed to make a turn, and without warning or giving a signal, she would whip the car around the corner. Somehow, I managed to follow her in spite of her lack of driving skills, and we arrived at her house. It was dark and very quiet and it appeared that no one was there. I felt relieved.

When we got in the house, I could see my army picture displayed on one end of a mantle, on the other end was a picture of Ruth when she was in her early twenties. No other picture was displayed—none of my three brothers and no other family members. Aunt Ocala did not care for dark-skinned people so the picture of her light-skinned grand was the only one on display.

Ruth went into the boy's room and found many of Ocala's personal papers opened on the dresser. She brought them out to where I was sitting in the little den just off the kitchen.

"Auntie," Ruth shouted. "They know all of your business. They know everything you got."

Ruth took the papers from one of the envelopes. It revealed that Ocala had more than $5,000.00 in a checking account, and much more than that in a money market account.

Ocala indicated that she had no idea that she had that much in either account. I couldn't believe what I was seeing and hearing. Now I could see why the grandchildren were waiting. With that much money they could continue not working much longer!

We finally finished at Ocala's. I was ready to leave when I first got there and was eager to hit the road back to Raleigh, but first I had to drop Ruth off at her hotel room. Although she had taken a taxi several times to and from the hotel, she had no idea which exit would take us to the hotel. After driving back and forth for at least 45 minutes, we were finally there. We sat in the car, conversing for a while. It was seldom that we got to talk one-on-one.

"Ruth, you know why we don't stay in touch with Aunt Ocala, don't you? You see, Daddy told us that he dropped out of school to help her go to college and she looked down on him because he never finished high school. Daddy never got over that and neither did we."

"I know, Frank," Ruth replied. "But you don't know the half of it!"

I thought I knew the whole story, and didn't know if I was ready for more.

"What are you talking about?" I asked with reluctance.

"Frank, Aunt Ocala never thought that your mother was worthy of marrying into the family!" Ruth responded.

"What? My mother wasn't what?" I asked in amazement.

"That's right, Frank. Aunt Ocala didn't want your father to marry your mother, and she let him know how she felt."

I was sorry that I had ever agreed to be co-executor with Ruth now, but I had promised Ruth that I would and I try to keep promises.

"You know Aunt Ocala was always into status and skin color. She wasn't too happy when my father married my mother either. You know how dark my mother was." Ruth's mother had died a couple of months earlier and had very dark skin.

"I can't believe that shit!" I replied.

"Well, it's true, Frank. You mean you never knew that?"

"Never," I replied. I can't describe how I felt.

"You know, Ruth, maybe all of the hell Ocala is catching is her just reward."

"My mother always said that she would pay for her evil ways, and now it looks as though she is," Ruth responded.

"Damn! Well, I guess I better get on down this road. I love you, Ruth."

"Same here, babe. Drive safely, and thanks."

I kissed Ruth on the cheek and don't remember much about the trip back to Raleigh, but I was relieved to finally know the whole truth. Just two months later, Uncle Edward passed and three months later Aunt Ocala passed. I couldn't make her funeral and I didn't feel bad about it either.

CHAPTER 4

I never knew my grandfather on my mother's side. I did know my grandmother and she, like my grandfather Joshua, was mean. Her name was Emma Pauline Smalls. I always felt that she hated me because of my light skin. And maybe I didn't like her because of her dark skin and her mean ways. I never heard her say anything nice and she was one of the meanest persons I ever met. I mean, mean! She was even meaner that Joshua. I wrote the poem below about her.

"My grandmother had fat lips and I hated her.

My grandmother had kinky hair, and I hated her.

My grandmother had a wide nose, and I hated her.

My grandmother was dark as the darkest night, and I hated her.

For I learned the truth too late to love."

She had moved from Charleston and now lived in Harlem, New York. Many people from Charleston, and other parts of the South, had migrated to New York where being black wasn't as difficult. Grandmother Smalls had thirteen children.

My mother was the oldest child. All but three of

her siblings died before my mother was eighteen. The other three all died tragically: George, a Korean War veteran, who was a heavy drinker, hemorrhaged to death; Dan, a veteran of the U.S. Navy, drowned under suspicious circumstances; and her sister Thelma, like her brother George, virtually drank herself to death. I could not imagine losing so many brothers and sisters and still being strong. Maybe Mama was just good at hiding her pain. My mother died in 1985, shortly after her sister Thelma died. It seemed like one of Mama's main purposes was to take care of her siblings. Of course, she also took real good care of Daddy, my brothers and me.

Thelma also had thirteen children, some of whom seemed slightly retarded from eating lead paint that had fallen from the walls of their decrepit, slummy apartment. The apartment smelled of old urine, the plumbing seldom worked, and it seemed like one twenty-five watt light bulb provided all of the lighting. I never looked forward to visiting them.

Some of Thelma's daughters also had several children. Some of them would also live under the same conditions under which they had grown up. My favorite among Thelma's children was Johnny. He was so nice and so talented. But in spite of all of the things that I remember about Johnny, his funeral probably had the greatest impact on me. I remember it just like it happened yesterday.

It was Thursday and I had just finished classes for

the day at Harvard. I went home and relaxed for a moment and then the phone rang. It was my mother.

"Frank, I need you to meet me in New York on Saturday morning. Johnny died and they gonna bury him on Saturday at 11:00 in the morning."

"Johnny died? What did he die of?"

"I don't know all that yet. Maybe we will find out when we get there."

"Where do you want me to come?"

"Meet me at Helen's." Helen was one of my cousins who had a serious hearing problem.

"You know how to get there, right?"

"Yes, ma'am. I'll check on the trains and I'll be there Friday night early."

"Okay. How is the family?"

"Everyone is okay."

"That's good. Tell them I said hi. I'll see you on Friday then."

"Okay, Momma."

Damn, Johnny had died! He was a nice dude. He could take a comic book and draw any character, capturing every detail. Johnny could draw just as good, if not better, than Stan Lee, who drew some of those comic books characters.

Johnny was one of the youngest of Thelma's 13 children. There was talk among the family when I was growing up that Thelma had so many children to get more welfare money. I never remember her ever having a job, but she always had a pint of Scotch Whiskey and was quick to offer you a drink.

Johnny was always quiet. He seemed to always be thinking when he wasn't drawing. Once he was visiting us in Charleston at my parents' house.

"Frank, do you like me?" Johnny asked me, looking me right in my eyes.

"Yes, Johnny, I do like you," I replied.

"Do you love me?"

"Yes, I love you, Johnny."

Johnny smiled. It seemed that no one had ever told him that before.

I caught an early evening train and arrived in 'The Big Apple' around 6 o'clock. Uncle Robbie, Helen's brother, and my mother's second cousin picked me up. They acted like sisters and brothers. Helen had all kinds of food. Momma, my brother, Buck and Helen were there when we got there. We ate, told jokes, and watched a little television until around 1 in the morning.

We got up the next morning around 7 and Robbie came over and took us to Thelma's apartment on 155th Street near Amsterdam Avenue. The elevator was broken, as usual, and we had to walk up five flights of stairs. I was concerned about my mom having to walk up all those steps, and it was unlikely that the elevator would be working after the funeral.

The strong odor of urine and cigarette smoke clung to the walls and steps like they, too, lived there. It was also dark as hell. Every other 40-watt bulb was either out or flickering. We made it to the 5th floor and now it was down the hall to Thelma's.

The door to her apartment was ajar, so we let ourselves in. The smell of the apartment reminded me of the stairwells, only fainter.

"Thelma! Anybody home?" Momma yelled.

"That y'all, Tavie?" Thelma yelled back.

"Yeah."

"Y'all come on back."

Momma led the way, followed by Helen, Uncle Robbie, Buck and me. I didn't want to be here. We moved slowly down the dark hallway. The only light was provided through an opaque window in the bathroom. We could smell the bathroom long before we got to it. It reminded me of the trip up the stairs, minus the cigarettes. I glanced into the bathroom. The wooden seat had a huge crack in it and was covered with urine-stained toilet tissue, and it looked like the toilet had never been cleaned. The tub had a ring around it that looked more like tar from the apparent accumulation of dead skin and dirt. A huge rust stain covered the entire bottom. I could not imagine anyone taking a bath in that tub. It made our little bathroom look like paradise!

We finally made it to the back of the apartment where Thelma and most of her children just sat or stood around like they were in somewhat of a daze. They didn't appear to be that sad, though; more stunned.

"It sure is good to see y'all," Thelma yelled. She

gave us all big, sweaty hugs. Thelma was always neatly dressed and had these huge dimples in her cheeks. She always had a bit of sweat on her face as it was always hot and stuffy in the apartment.

"Y'all get something to eat," she yelled. I looked at Momma and Buck.

Small cockroaches crawled all over the walls, obviously undisturbed by our presence. The children took turns keeping the roaches off of the table where the food lay that neighbors had brought in a show of sympathy. There was macaroni and cheese, greens, fried chicken, potato salad, green beans and iced tea. The smell of the food made the smell of the urine less powerful. The food looked good, but I was glad that Helen had cooked us a big breakfast.

I sat next to Tyrone, one of Johnny's brothers, who was about a year older than Johnny.

"I was out here with Johnny when he died, you know, Frank?"

"Really? What happened?"

"Johnny started talkin' bout how his stomach was hurtin' him real bad, so after a week we took him to the clinic. The people at the clinic told us that there wasn't nothing they could do for Johnny. So, we brought Johnny home. That night Johnny started to cry real bad, sayin' that his stomach was hurtin' real bad. We couldn't do nothin'. He kept crying and yellin' cause it was hurtin' him real bad. Sometimes he would cry himself to sleep. He woke up again and said that it was real bad and started cryin' and everything for about an hour. Then, he went back to sleep and the next morning he was dead. I knew he was dead when he went to sleep that last time cause he made a funny sound while he was sleepin'. He don't have to suffer no more now, though. He don't have to suffer no more."

"So, you were right there with him?"

"Right there with him until he died. Sure was."

Helen sort of felt that the boys would try to use the excuse of not having a dress shirt to keep from going to the funeral, so she had gone by a discount store the day before and bought enough shirts for everyone. The only problem was that she had only bought one size—16x34, and the largest boy probably needed a 14 ½x30! They complained, but Helen made them put those over-sized shirts on anyway. They really looked funny. Some of the collars were almost halfway down their chests, but no one laughed out of respect for Johnny.

The church was right around the corner, so we walked. The funeral was held in a small chapel and you could tell that not much thought and planning had gone into Johnny's funeral. There were only family members there. There was no program to hand out and the entire ceremony seemed more like a formality than a ceremony. I was glad when it was over.

We left the church and rode in an old family car to the gravesite. Rides to graveyards in New York seem to last forever. It seems like it is always cloudy and no one seems to respect the dead as they pass by. In The South, it is not uncommon for people to stop their cars, get out, and almost stand at attention until the funeral procession passes. In my experience with New York funerals, the entire funeral party seldom arrives intact as someone usually gets lost.

We finally arrived at the gravesite. The undertaker opened the back of the hearse and I just knew that his brothers would carry Johnny's body to the grave. Then, suddenly, this dirty, old white dude rode up on a yellow highlift like my father used to operate on his job at the Shipyard, and positioned it near the back door of the hearse. He slid the flat bars into the hearse and lifted Johnny's coffin out of the hearse with the fork-lift. He clumsily transported it to the grave and placed it on the belts that would lower his young body into its final resting place, away from friends and family.

The funeral director gave each of us a wilted red rosebud, which appeared to have been cut the day be-fore, but had obviously never been placed in water. After a brief prayer by the minister, Johnny's body was lowered into the grave. Each of us threw a rose on top of Johnny's coffin. Two sticks, which resembled huge Popsicle sticks, would mark Johnny's grave. I couldn't believe what I was witnessing. Johnny always won-dered if he was loved. I wondered if his question had finally been answered.

CHAPTER 5

My grandmother would visit us at least twice a year. My father never looked forward to her coming and neither did my brothers or me. She seemed to suffer from several illnesses including asthma and a heart condition. We were often awakened by her loud moaning late at night from the various pains that tormented her.

"I eee, I eee," she would moan. I will never forget those sounds.

She would always come to visit us by train. It was fun seeing the trains, but I didn't look forward to seeing her. Her meanness and moans haunted me. One day, we went to pick her up in a wooden box. The box contained her body. She had died in New York and her body was shipped to Charleston for burial. I have not forgotten that. I was sad for my mother, but I wasn't really sad. I had seen her viciously beat my cousin, Sammy, with her fists as she held his head between her huge legs. I had never seen anyone beaten like that!

She never touched me, but I feared her! I never

got the chance to tell her that I loved her and she never told me that she loved me either. I will never forget that at her funeral, they placed all of her eyeglasses and her medicines in the coffin with her. That was a custom in those days, as the old folks believed that the dead would still need their medicines and glasses even after death.

Our street was a dead-end dirt street. There were about fifteen houses. It was a typical working-class neighborhood. My father and at least three other men worked at the Charleston Naval Shipyard. Many of the black men in Charleston worked at the Shipyard.

Mr. Noel, our next door neighbor, whom we seldom saw, drove a tractor-trailer. Mr. Jimmy, our neighbor across the street, worked at the local Coburg Dairy, which was about two blocks away. His wife, Miss Nellie, spent most of her time sitting on their porch. She had a badly swollen leg and couldn't work. She was kind of mean. She would always yell and fuss at us when our ball went into her yard.

One of our neighbors drove a cab, another worked at a men's clothing store, one was a nurse, my mother and a couple of other women worked at the American Tobacco Factory, and a few were on welfare.

A lady named Miss Butler lived in the house on the corner, right next to our house. In those days, her house was considered to be a small mansion. She reminded me of Mary Poppins—always neatly dressed and carrying a parasol. She acted like she never wanted to speak to any of us "common" folks. Her house had the only garage in the entire neighborhood.

We played a lot of stickball and quite often our ball would wind up in her backyard. She would not let us come into her yard to retrieve it. Sometimes we would jump over her fence and get it and if she saw us, she would threaten to call the police. None of us liked her.

Another lady lived in the house—the Widow Dart. That's how everyone referred to her. I never saw her outside of the house. Sometimes when we were sitting on our porch, which faced her window, we would catch her staring at us. When we would catch sight of her, she would quickly close the curtains. She was very pale, looked like she had never been in the sun, and appeared ghost-like. It was very eerie catching her watching us. We probably saw her less than ten times in over ten years!

There was a library for blacks on the corner of Bogard and Kracke Streets, across from where Miss Butler and the Widow Dart lived. The building was called Dart's Hall Library. It was a huge, gray, two-story, wood-framed building. Most of the paint was peeling. It had about ten fairly large rooms, but most of the rooms were empty and smelled of mildew. I heard that the building was used as a dance hall before it was converted to a library.

It was named after the Widow Dart's family and only contained about one-hundred books. Blacks were not allowed to use the huge, well-lighted, and well-equipped so-called public libraries. I spent a lot of time in Dart's Hall Library, however, and probably read all of the books. I read many books on animal husbandry, and some on the great boxers and baseball players. Perhaps, the library was my sanctity from the cruel world outside its walls.

The Murrays lived across the street from the library. Mrs. Bert Murray owned the house. She was a renowned educator and an extremely kind person. Her daughter, Hazel, who was my high school math teacher, and her husband Jimmy, a local radio personality, shared the house with Mrs. Murray. They were the only college-educated persons in the neighborhood. I never knew if Miss Butler or the Widow Dart had finished college, as they stayed to themselves and had nothing to do with the other people in the neighborhood. They lived in the community, but were not a part of it.

For the most part, we were a close-knit community and no one ever had to lock their doors. I guess this was one of the true examples of community watch. We always were playing football or baseball and the adults would sit in front of their yards and cheer us on. Mr. Henry who worked at a men's clothing store, sold snow cones and others would eat watermelon and drink lemonade to cool off. Sandlot teams from other neighborhoods would come to challenge us in football and baseball, but we never lost a game! We called ourselves the Kracke Court Sluggers.

There was Buck and myself, the twins—Ronald and Raymond Gadson, Jerry Devore, Hercules Hunter, Black Luke (Phillip Lucas), Thelly (a tomboy whose last name I never knew), Nathaniel Jenkins, Doug (Douglas Ashley), Sweety (Bernard Jamison), and Coffee (Alvin Thompson). I was the only light-skinned one in the bunch, but no one seemed to care. We were always hanging out together, but we knew that when the street light came on, everyone had to go home. There were no exceptions.

Daddy had put a basketball goal in our yard, but we preferred football and baseball. We also boxed a lot. We always had a set of boxing gloves. We got a nice set one Christmas and took real good care of them.

One day, this older guy, Doug's brother, Walter, insisted on boxing with me. He was about eighteen and I was twelve. His nickname was "Heart," because he had a bad heart. We seldom saw him. I told him that I didn't want to fight him, but he started taunting me and asking me if I was afraid to fight him. I looked at Buck and he kinda gave me a signal to go ahead.

I really didn't want to fight him. He was much older than I was and he was also bigger and taller. I could tell that he really didn't know how to box though and I used that to my advantage. I put a good whipping on him and tried to stop several times, but he wouldn't let me.

"Come on, you scared? He would yell.

"I don't want to fight you no more," I pleaded.

"Come on, red boy. Fight me!" He yelled again.

I continued to beat up on him and he began to breathe real hard, but he kept trying. Finally, I took off my gloves and walked away, leaving him almost breathless and totally embarrassed. He eventually caught his breath and slowly walked home. I felt bad for him, but I had told him that I didn't want to fight.

Later on that evening we got the word that Walter had died. I felt responsible, although all of my friends were telling me that I had given him the chance to quit and he wouldn't.

We went by his house that was just around the corner on Bogard Street next to Miss Butler's house and whose backyard backed up to our side yard. Walter's body was lying on a couch with a rag tied around his head to keep his jaw closed, waiting on the undertaker to pick him up. That was an eerie feeling seeing him just lying there and knowing that earlier we had just boxed. I felt that if I had stopped fighting him much sooner, he might still be alive. That feeling haunted me for a long time; at times, I still think of that day as if it was yesterday. I didn't enjoy boxing too much after that.

The Iceman, the Watermelon Man, the Rag Man, and the Ice Cream Man visited our community just about everyday. The Iceman would use his ice pick and break up some ice for us to cool off with. Most of us had iceboxes.

We didn't get a refrigerator until I was about twelve. A twelve-pound block of ice cost twelve cents.

Just about every yard had some kind of fruit tree in it. We had two fig trees and a mulberry tree in our backyard and a plum tree in our side yard. One of the largest pecan trees I have ever seen stood proudly right across the street from our house in front of one of the vacant lots and right next on the corner of Mr. Jimmy and Miss Nellie's yard. We never wanted for enough pecans.

We spent many hours under that tree, seeking shade and just having fun. Eventually, Hurricane Hazel came along and really hurt that tree. It was never the same. It still produced some pecans, but not many. Miss Murray's house on the corner had some of the sweetest Japanese Plums one could ever want to taste. The limbs hung over the sidewalk and you could feast whenever you wanted to.

I also raised chickens. I had about twenty-five hens and three roosters. One of my friends, Levon, and I would ride our bikes through town and if I saw a chicken that I wanted, I would just ring the person's doorbell and ask them if they would sell it to me. Most of them did. I would also have to catch the chicken. I usually paid about $3.00 for each chicken. To make sure that the chicken didn't fly out of the yard, I would cut the end off of a few of its feathers. The feathers would grow back, but by the time they did, the chicken was usually used to its new home and wouldn't try to leave.

Levon really got me interested in raising chickens. His mother had some beautiful chickens in their backyard and he basically took care of them. Many people raised chickens.

I would also buy baby chicks from Week's Feed Store on Spring Street, which was just around the corner from our house and right next to the Ice House. I had a hen that was very special that I named "Shorty." She was a Brahma and also a setting hen. A setting hen would sit on her nest for twenty-one days with little food or water until the eggs had hatched. I would collect eggs from several of the other hens and place them in Shorty's nest when it was obvious that she was ready to set. As a result, I would have about five different breeds being hatched by Shorty. She treated them all as if they were her own. Shorty was my favorite chicken. I considered her to be one of my friends.

One day, my brother John went into my chicken yard and set this heavy iron pot on a stick that was attached to a string. He put some chicken feed under the huge pot and eventually some of the chickens, including Shorty, came under the pot to eat. John yanked the string and the huge pot came crashing down. All of the chickens escaped, except Shorty. She almost made it, but the huge pot caught one of her legs, and broke it. When I learned what had happened I tried to tend to her leg as best as I could. I got two Popsicle sticks and placed them on her leg and secured them with some cloth. The leg eventually healed, but now Shorty had a distinct limp. I never forgave John for that, although I knew that he didn't mean to hurt her.

I also had a large Rhode Island Red rooster that I named "Big Red." I raised him from a chick. He was the biggest rooster I have ever seen. He was a watch rooster. If someone Big Red didn't know entered the chicken yard, Big Red would circle the person and then jump up on the person's chest and hit the person with both spurs while he pecked at the person with his large beak. He was truly a proud bird.

Big Red would always get out of the yard, walking on the top of the fences that connected neighbor's yards, and visit other hens in the neighborhood. I kept telling Big Red to be careful, but to no avail. One Thanksgiving season, Big Red wandered off and I never saw him again. I couldn't imagine anyone trying to eat him for Thanksgiving dinner because his meat must have been tough.

I had White Leghorns, Barred Rocks, Brahmas, Rhode Island Reds, New Hampshire Reds, Gamecocks, and even two Bantams. I had also developed some hybrids from cross breeding. One of my hybrids was a pure gray chicken with a dark red comb. It was a cross of a White Leghorn and a Barred Rock. My chickens laid many eggs and I would sell some of them to Mrs. Murray to help me buy chicken feed. We ate the rest. Mama made some of her best cakes with fresh eggs from our backyard.

Eventually, Levon became jealous of my success

with my chickens and he went into my chicken yard one day and took a brick and broke all of the eggs that were in the nests. I never confronted him because I didn't see him do it, but I could tell that he had done it. I never told anyone else about it. That incident ended our friendship, if we ever had one.

I just loved sitting in our backyard with my chickens. They would just walk around me like I wasn't even there, although Shorty would always look at me as if to acknowledge my presence. They didn't care whether I had light skin and freckles. Sometimes, I would sit there for hours, just watching them and being at total peace.

The lady whose house backed up to my chicken yard didn't like my chickens. She complained that they smelled. I could understand that and tried very hard to keep the yard as clean as possible.

Early one morning, a pack of stray dogs broke into my chicken yard and killed most of my chickens. She heard the commotion and listened to it for more than an hour, but did not call us until most of my chickens had been slaughtered. Shorty had been killed too. Some of those that survived had huge teeth marks on their bodies. I will never forget pulling the skin back on one of my surviving hens and seeing maggots eating at her flesh beneath the wound.

I never forgave her for that. I went away to college the next year and left my remaining chickens under the care of my baby brother, John. That was the end of my chickens.

CHAPTER 6

We would play cowboys and Indians all of the time. Of course, the cowboys would always win because that was always how it was in the movies. We spent many weekends at the movies. There were two black movie theaters—the Lincoln and the Palace. They were both owned and operated by blacks. They were diagonally across from each other on King Street near Spring Street.

On our way to the movies, we would always stop by Taylor's Bakery, a black-owned bakery on Spring Street near King Street, and just around the corner from the theaters. Mr. Taylor had a fine bakery. He would always be in the bakery and always had flour all over him. He was a very nice man. Mr. Taylor provided the wedding cakes for all of the black weddings and also sold some of his pastries through some of the black-owned corner stores. Sometimes you could get his pastries still warm in some of the corner grocery stores if you happened to be there when they were delivered fresh from his bakery. There was a little store on just about every corner in the black neighborhood and most of them were owned and operated by blacks. In most cases, the owners lived upstairs just above the store and steps were located in the back of the store for access to the two floors.

Mr. Taylor also sold bags of crumbs for 10 cents. Grease-stained small, brown paper bags were filled with broken doughnuts, pieces of cinnamon rolls and other pastries, and pieces of cake that did not meet Mr. Taylor's high standards of perfection. They were so good! We would sneak the bags into the theater and munch on them through most of the movie.

The Lincoln Theater was the most popular and you could see a double feature with at least three cartoons for 10 cents! If you had a dollar, you could pay for the movie, buy a hot dog, a soda, popcorn, and a candy bar, and still have enough money to buy ice cream when you got out. We saw a lot of cowboy movies: Hopalong Cassidy, Lash LaRue, Tim Holt, Roy Rogers, The Cisco Kid, Randolph Scott, Johnny Mack Brown and many others. All the cowboys had beautiful horses. My favorite was Trigger, Roy Rogers' horse. We also saw many Tarzan (the King of the Jungle) movies. Tarzan movies had a powerful influence on shaping the image of blacks, but most of us did not realize it at the time.

The cartoons were usually Donald Duck, Mickey Mouse, Felix the Cat, the Roadrunner, Popeye, and Woody Woodpecker.

Going to the movies was a bittersweet experience

for me. I loved being there with my friends. On the other hand, most people urinated in the aisles from their seats because the bathrooms were filthy. So the theater smelled of urine, popcorn and hot dogs. Huge roaches and rats crawled around freely.

Another thing that I hated was that after each roll of film had run out they would cut the lights on until the next reel was installed. This would take several minutes, although it seemed longer. They would take their time changing the reels so that everyone could go to the concession stand. That is when many eyes focused on me.

"Look at that white boy! What is he doing here?" I would hear some of them yell. That hurt so much. Sometimes, although I felt like some candy or popcorn, I would remain in my seat. I did this most of the time. I would hear their ignorant taunting as I walked to and from the concession stand. Most of the time, I would just ask one of my friends to buy food for me when they went to get some.

The Palace usually wasn't as crowded and I would sometimes go there and sit in the back by myself and enjoy a movie without being harassed. I liked going to the movies, but usually couldn't wait to get back on Kracke Street! No one taunted me there.

We made slingshots out of tree branches, the tongue out of pair of old leather shoes, and rubber from an old inner tube. Sometimes, we would have slingshot battles using Chinaberries as ammo. We played rough and dangerously, but somehow no one ever got seriously hurt. They say that the Lord looks out for fools and babies, and He sure looked out for us.

We would also sneak through The Citadel (a military college that was right next to my high school) to access a nice creek where we would swim and catch crabs with chicken necks tied on a string. Blacks couldn't attend The Citadel. I would later learn that the Citadel was established in response to a planned slave revolt organized by Denmark Vesey. Vesey was also the pastor of Emanuel AME Church which sat on that property before it was burned to the ground by angry whites. Mother Emanuel was rebuilt on Calhoun Street. A "house negro" told "massa" and undermined the plot and Vesey was hung.

We would get these evil stares from the white cadets like they really wanted to harm us. They could never catch us though. We were always one step ahead of them. We would sell some of the crabs in the neighborhood. What we didn't sell we would eat ourselves. We would make a fire in my backyard and cook them in a big iron pot that was used to boil clothes to make them clean—the same pot that had broken Shorty's leg.

We ate lots of crabs. All of us could swim. Charleston was surrounded by water on three sides, so knowing how to swim was required for survival. Most of us learned to swim in the black pool at

Harmon Field where they also had a tennis court, a basketball court, swings, slides, a small recreation center, a football field and a baseball field. We spent a lot of time there. We were not allowed to go to any of the white-only parks that always had the better facilities.

Harmon Field is where Buck and I first played organized baseball. Our Little League was all black, as was the Pony League across town at Martin Park. Most of the teams were sponsored by local black businesses such as the funeral homes and some of the stores. The Police Department and the Pan Hellenic Council also sponsored teams.

All of the baseball leagues for boys older than 15, such as Babe Ruth and American Legion, were closed to blacks. The only chance blacks had to play beyond the age of 15 was to play in high school or play on a sandlot team. Burke High School was the only school in the area with a baseball team. I played there. Many good baseball players never got to reach their full potential because there was just nowhere for them to play.

Buck and I played Pony League baseball with the Hawks at Martin Park at the foot of the Cooper River Bridge, which connects Charleston with Mount Pleasant. It was hard for anyone from our side of town to play "across" town. Most of the players on the Hawks were from our neighborhood. We had a good team, and won some championships. Sometimes, we would have to run back home after a game, because we were from "across town" and many of the kids did not like us, especially after we beat them in a game. Our manager was Mr. Lawrence who worked at the cigar factory with my mother. The league folded from a lack of money so I wasn't able to play my last year. I was just beginning to fully develop my baseball skills. I would not be able to play organized ball until I transferred to Burke High School.

Buck and I made Burke High School's baseball team. Buck only got the chance to play his senior year and I played for two years. Buck received scholarships to play baseball and football from Delaware State College in Dover, Delaware. They also gave him an academic scholarship. He had the highest batting average in the nation in 1965, but was never drafted. One major league scout told Buck that he was an excellent ball player, but he was too old and too black! He was 21 (too old), and was known to speak his mind (too black). I am also sure that his active participation in the Civil Rights movement in 1963 didn't help either. Maybe he should have not gone with me to integrate Folly Beach.

I got an academic scholarship to Saint Augustine's College in Raleigh, North Carolina. They didn't have a baseball team, so I attempted to transfer to Delaware State but it didn't work out. Delaware State's Registrar lost all of my application materials so I never got the chance to play beyond high school.

I really didn't like going to the Harmon Field Pool,

though. The children would always tease me about my light skin and called me names such as "white boy" and "cracker boy." Many of them would also try to pick fights with me. I had the toughest brother in town, though, and Buck would always rescue me when I needed help, but he couldn't shield me from the verbal abuse. I would try to stay in the water with just my head exposed.

Usually, when we left the pool, we would stop by Scotty's, one of the corner stores right across from Burke High School, and get a greasy link sausage smothered in mustard for 15 cents. They were so good, and the greasier they were, the better they seemed to taste. They were almost burnt on one side and that made it taste even better.

CHAPTER 7

We lived about fifteen minutes from the Atlantic Ocean and the beach, but we had to drive about one and a half hours to go to one of the black beaches. There were Atlantic Beach, Beaufort Beach, and McKenzie Beach for blacks. There was also Riverside Beach, which wasn't really a beach, but more like a creek that was just across the Cooper River Bridge. The only time you could really swim was when the tide was high. The water was usually full of broken bottles. Buck jumped into the water and got cut real bad by a broken bottle that someone had thrown in the water.

I liked the beach, but hated to go because I stood out like a sore thumb among all the dark-skinned blacks. I got stared at from the other children as if they were questioning why I was there when I could go to my own beach. I would usually try to stay in the water with just my head showing so that they couldn't see me that well, but eventually I had to come out of the water, and then the cruel stares penetrated me like hot swords.

Mama would get up early in the morning and fry a lot of her love-laced chicken, and make some macaroni and cheese, and some red rice. She would also prepare bread pudding for dessert. She would also make some lemonade and iced tea. She would wrap all of the food up in newspaper and then place them in large, brown grocery bags. This kept the food nice and warm.

We would try to arrive at the beach early enough so that we could find a nice parking place with some shade, but still close to the water. We would usually play in the water until about noon and then it was time to eat some of Mama's love-laced food! Everyone brought their own food because blacks were not allowed to buy from any of the little restaurants along the highway. We couldn't even stop to use the rest rooms. We had to stop along the side of the road to relieve ourselves. That really didn't sit well with my mother.

I remember how the white highway patrolmen would always harass the men, including my father, at the beaches. They would search their cars, and make them start up their cars to see if they were "too loud." Some of the men would be arrested if the cops thought that they were drunk. Getting home without a ticket was also difficult as the cops would routinely stop a car full of blacks and harass them. Just about all of the men drank at the beach and the cops couldn't wait to make them walk the white line in the middle of the road. If you could walk the line, you would be let go; if not, you had to pay a fine or go to jail if you didn't have the fine money. Daddy could always walk that line!

We would usually get back from the beach around nine o'clock and by the time everyone had taken a bath it was usually around eleven before we got to bed. Since we didn't have a hot water heater, we had to boil water for each bath and that made it even longer. Buck and I would always share the tub first, then Bobby and John, and then Mama and Daddy would take separate baths.

I remember our first experience with a shower when we were visiting my cousin Dot in Long Island, New York. Daddy had never used a shower before and he panicked and almost drowned. He was slapping the water away from his face with his hands, trying to breathe as the water splashed on him. That was too funny!

CHAPTER 8

Life was real good in the arms of Kracke Court. However, it wasn't good when I left her. In Kracke Court, I was just Frank. Outside of Kracke Court, I was called all kinds of names. I will never forget the day that I was on the other end of Kracke Street when I encountered these two guys who had just gotten out of the Army.

"Look at that Cracker Boy," one of them yelled.

"Hey, Cracker Boy," the other one said.

I just looked away and dropped my head.

"You know why you look so white, Cracker Boy? The milkman screwed your mama. That's why you look so white Cracker Boy."

I felt so confused. No one had ever talked to me that harshly before. I wondered if they might be telling the truth. After all, I was different. All of my brothers looked like they were black. I would later learn that they called me that name because I was the color of a Saltine Cracker. I had often heard blacks refer to whites as crackers, and now I was being called one, too. I hurt inside. Every time I saw those two guys I would try to avoid them, but every time they saw me they would yell out "Hey, Cracker Boy."

For some reason, both of those guys died tragically at very young ages. I can't say that I was happy, but I can say that I wasn't sad.

People always dropped by our house. Daddy and Momma had lots of friends who would stop by, especially on Saturdays. Most of the men who came by were looking for a drink of whiskey or some of Mama's potent homemade wine. Daddy had this one friend who walked with a limp that Daddy called Dollar Bill. He would always tease me.

"Who is that brass ankle, you got there, Bill?" he would ask my father.

My father would just brush it off, but he never told the man to stop. Daddy obviously didn't know how much it was hurting me, as I am sure that if he had known, he would have stopped it. I also tried to act like it wasn't bothering me.

He was referring to me and would look at me with this hateful grin. He thought it was funny, but I didn't. A "brass ankle" was a light-skinned offspring of a Native American woman and a white man. Every time he saw me he would call me a brass ankle. To avoid the pain, I would usually go outside each time I saw him at the door.

To add to my confusion, when I got my driver's license, they had my race listed as "white." You didn't have to put your race on the application form. They would just look at you and make that determination. I was so excited about getting my license until I saw "white." Thank God that I never had to use it, so the only ones who knew were my family. It was our secret.

CHAPTER 9

For some reason, my mother decided that we should all attend the private Catholic school, Immaculate Conception (ICS), on Coming Street. The school went from kindergarten through twelfth grade. The school had three floors with the lower classes taught on the lower floors and the upper classes taught on the second and third floors.

All of the teachers were black nuns from the Oblate Sisters of Providence out of Baltimore, Maryland. Most of them were very beautiful. They all lived in a convent downtown, which was headed by two white priests. Even at a very young age that bothered me. I couldn't really figure it out, but I knew that something wasn't quite right with that. Most of the students who attended ICS were Catholic and most of them had light skin like me. I always knew the pain of having light skin, but now I would also feel the pain of being a protestant in a Catholic School. Maybe my mother sent all of us there to protect me, but it didn't shield me from the pain.

Most of the students there were also members of

Jack and Jill, a social club for "certain" children. I had heard about this so-called elite club, but had never paid it much attention. Then, one day, it all became quite clear. One of my friends, Delbert Woods, asked me if I would like to come to a Jack and Jill party. I said that I might wish to. He then said that I could bring someone with me if I wanted to and I said that I did.

"Who will you bring?" asked Delbert.

"Jerry Devore," I replied.

"You can't bring him!" he almost shouted.

"Why?" I inquired.

"He's too dark," replied Delbert.

"Then I won't be coming."

"Fine."

That little exchange completely changed the way I related to Delbert and most of the other light-skinned children from that day on. I couldn't bring my best friend to a Jack and Jill party because he was too dark! I was confused. I knew that most of the light-skinned people had their own neighborhoods and even their own schools and churches; now I learned that they also had their own clubs. You could join Jack and Jill if you weren't light-skinned, but only if your parents were professionals such as teachers, doctors, or lawyers.

I began to realize now why I was so despised by some of the darker skinned blacks. Many of them probably thought that I was like many of the other light-skinned children—thinking that my light skin made me better than them. In my case, that was far from the truth!

Jerry Devore was my best friend and I hung out with him most of the time. He had very dark skin. Maybe being seen with him validated my blackness, but I really did like him. He lived diagonally across the street from us. His parents were very strict and seldom let him come out to play with us. Much of the time he would just stand in his yard behind the fence and watch us play.

Most of us would meet on the corner of Ashley Avenue and Bogard Street in the afternoons, just outside the corner grocery store which was owned by an elderly Greek guy who lived over the store with his wife and son. These were the only whites in our neighborhood and you only saw them when you went into the store. They sold meats, canned goods, bread and all kinds of candy and cookies that you could buy for a penny a piece. Some were two for a penny. They also sold kerosene as most people in the neighborhood had kerosene heaters. The store usually smelled of kerosene, meat and cookies.

We would usually buy a bag of chips and a soda, which sold for around fifteen cents for both. We also liked the sliced luncheon meat that we could buy for about ten cents (about 4 slices), and eat it with some cinnamon rolls that cost about a dime for a three-roll pack. We used to call that "flying a kite." I don't know why, though. Sometimes we would find some old soda bottles and sell them for a penny apiece and scrape up enough money to "fly a kite." All sodas came in glass bottles and you could sell them at the corner stores for a penny while the larger grocery stores would give you two cents.

I, as well of some of my friends, had paper routes. One guy delivered prescriptions for the drug store, some worked at corner stores, and others did odd jobs like raking leaves to get some money. I also shined shoes at a barbershop operated by this real nice elderly man named "King." I got about 10 cents for a shine. If I brushed the hair from the customers after their haircuts they might give me a nickel tip. Most of them didn't give me anything. I also ran errands for Mr. King such as picking up his lunch from one of the local restaurants. He would let me keep all of the money I earned. The men were always telling jokes and I liked that.

Once, when I was shining this man's shoes he asked me if I had any elbow grease. I told him that I didn't know what he was talking about and he told me to go across the street to the gas station and ask the guy if he would sell me some elbow grease. I did as he asked and learned that he was making a fool of me. When I got back to the shop, everyone was laughing. I didn't find it very funny. In a good week I could make two or three dollars.

I also delivered newspapers. I only made $3.00 a week doing that. I delivered the Charleston Evening Post. The morning paper was the News and Courier.

They sold for five cents and I usually delivered about 100 each day, except on Sunday. Many of my customers never paid me. On top of that, the newspaper company would force us to buy "extras" (extra newspapers), expecting us to sell them on the corner. Most of us got at about 20 extras that we had to pay for but most of the time couldn't sell.

The newspaper company would also take out $1.00 each week and "save" it for us. What they were really doing was ensuring that they would be paid. If a carrier did not pay the newspaper company the unpaid amount would be taken from the savings.

Our family visited New York each summer. Mama would save up enough money for gas, tolls, food and entertainment. It was amazing how she could do that. We would spend two weeks there and live with relatives. We might spend a few days with one relative and then spend the rest of the time with another. One of the things I enjoyed most was seeing all of the entertainers at the Apollo Theater in Harlem. We would plan our trips so that we would catch two full shows. The shows usually ran for one week and included a weekend show. We saw most of the top entertainers such as The Temptations, The Drifters, Sam and Dave, The Delfonics, The Coasters, The Four Tops, Stevie Wonder, Pigmeat Markham, Junior Walker and the Allstars, King Curtis, The Shirelles, James Brown, and numerous others. We saw just about every entertainer that we would hear on the radio.

We would also go to the Bronx Zoo and Coney Island. The zoo back home had no more than twenty different animals. The Bronx Zoo had every animal one could imagine. I loved going to New York. For two weeks out of every year the color of my skin didn't matter. There were dark-skinned people, light-skinned people and people from all over the world. You could eat in any restaurant and could sit downstairs in the movie theaters.

One summer when we went to New York, I asked my friend, Philip Lucas (Black Luke was his nickname), to handle my paper route. He had a good time. He failed to deliver the papers to some of my good customers. He also kept all of the money he collected and never paid the newspaper company. He bought himself some new clothes and really lived it up. The newspaper company took all of that money out of my savings. I had accumulated almost three hundred dollars and they took more than fifty of that.

I kept my route for about another year and made up for most of the money the company had taken. When I finally did quit, they gave me $250.00 in cash! That was big money in those days and it was the most money I had ever seen. On my way home I was trying to decide what I wanted to do with the money. I knew that Mama and Daddy were trying to save up enough money so that Mama could have her teeth fixed. As I approached my house, I could see Mama sitting on the upstairs porch. I went upstairs and gave her the entire

$250.00! I told her that it was for her teeth. I could see the joy on her face and especially in her eyes. I felt good too. Mama got her teeth fixed and could now smile with her mouth open.

CHAPTER 10

We would usually hang out on the corner until the streetlights came on, which was the signal for most of us that we at least had to check in with our moms. We could usually negotiate staying out longer as long as we were within yelling distance of our mom's voices.

Some of the guys could stay out as late as they wanted to, but for the rest of us, we knew that we had about a half hour to check in after the lights came on. If we failed to, our moms would send someone to look for us. If we couldn't be found or came in late, we might be grounded (not able to leave our own street). There was no discussion when you were grounded.

One night, as Jerry and I approached the corner of Kracke and Bogard Streets, we noticed my brother, Buck, sitting on the corner talking to a girl.

"What's up Buck?" I yelled.

"Nothin'," he replied.

The girl turned to Buck and asked, "Who is that white-looking guy?"

"Oh, he is just a friend of the family," Buck uttered.

That hurt. Jerry could see the pain in my face.

My own brother, my idol and hero, the only person I wanted to be just like, was denying his kinship to me. That was one of the most painful experiences I can recall other than the recent death of my grandmother and my parents some sixty years later.

I couldn't get to sleep that night. I had to get rid of my light skin. I wanted Buck to love me. I wanted him to be proud to tell everyone that I was his brother. At the time I didn't realize that he was also suffering from a similar confusion. He hated me because he was dark and I hated myself because I was light-skinned.

Most of the nuns were nice, but some of them were mean and bordered on being evil. I still remember being hit across my knuckles with the metal side of twelve-inch rulers and being slapped so hard that I thought that my face would fall off. There were only a few non-Catholics at ICS and we were constantly reminded of it. We were warned that we were doomed to the fiery pits of hell if we did not convert to Catholicism.

My parents paid a weekly tuition for us to attend ICS. My brothers and I were the only ones from our neighborhood that attended ICS. I would also learn later that many people believed that any Protestant who attended ICS thought that they were too good for the public schools, although I did not realize it at my young age. My brothers and I had no say-so in the matter. Mama wanted us to go there and that is where we went.

I made some friends at ICS, but I never really felt that I was fully accepted at the school. One of my closest friends was Arthur Lewis. Arthur was even lighter than me. He had sharp facial features and straight, sandy, brownish blonde hair. Anyone who didn't know him would think that he was white. He was not like the other light-skinned kids at ICS. I sensed that he liked me as a human being. Maybe Arthur made me feel more black.

Arthur lived on Race Street, which was about five blocks from my house, off Ashley Avenue, near Hampton Park. We often walked from school together. Most of us had book bags, which were similar to the backpacks kids use today, but they were army green and made of heavy canvas. They had arm straps so that they could be carried like backpacks. Although it was called a book bag, you could carry anything and everything in it—books, pencils, pens, crayons, toys, gadgets, and even one's lunch. A book bag usually smelled of canvas, paper, crayons, fruit, and peanut butter and jelly sandwiches.

In addition to carrying one's belongings, the book bag was also quite useful as a weapon. You would use it like you would use a pillow in a pillow fight, except it was heavier since it was full of your "stuff." This made it rather difficult to swing with any real force. Consequently, a book bag couldn't really hurt you; it just knocked you around a bit. Such fights were as common as "tag" and "hide and seek" and usually took place before and after school.

As Arthur and I were walking home one day, we began to have a friendly book bag fight about three blocks from my house on Rutledge Avenue near Bogard Street. I swung my bag at Arthur and he jumped off of the sidewalk between two parked cars to avoid the blow, almost going into the street.

He rebounded and was about to strike back when this huge black car screeched to a halt. The door on the passenger side swung open and a huge angry, red-faced white man leaned over from the driver's side, looked me right in the eyes and said, "Get in boy!"

I could see a huge gun on his side and a micro-phone and radio on the dashboard of his car so I assumed that he must be some sort of policeman. I was frightened and confused and could not figure out what he wanted with me.

Again, he yelled, "Get in boy!"

I remember me and my friends being harassed by the police just about every day. I remember how they would run us off of the street corners where we would just be standing around having some fun and how they would take away our roller skates if they caught us skating in places other than designated skating zones. These were usually many blocks from our neighborhoods where the streets weren't as smooth.

Everyone got a pair of roller skates for Christmas and we would skate from dawn to dusk, only taking breaks to go home and eat. The streets were gray with the steel dust from our skate wheels. We skated so much that we would have to put new wheels on after about three days. You could skate anywhere through New Year's Day, but then you were only allowed to skate on streets designated as skating zones. Our streets were never skating zones and we would have to go several blocks to the zone. The streets in the zone were too rough to skate on so we usually took a chance and skated on our own street anyway. If the cops caught you, they would take away your skates and there was nothing you could do about it. The cops seemed to enjoy doing this. I only had my skates taken away once. It was hard to escape on skates.

I really didn't want to get in any trouble so I slowly walked towards and car and slid onto the front seat beside the policeman. I was very frightened and a small teardrop landed on my upper lip.

"Boy you are in a heap of trouble," he growled.

"What.......what did.....I.......do?" I whispered.

My mouth was dry. I wanted to use the bathroom very badly. I wanted my mother.

The detective sped off with me in the car. I could see Arthur standing on the curb looking confused—the same way I must have looked over what was happening.

"You goin' to jail, boy," he yelled at the top of his voice.

"What did I do?" I asked in fear.

"Shut up! What's yo momma's name, boy?"

"Octavia Godfrey."

I could hardly talk I was so afraid. I had heard stories about young black boys who were killed by angry white men and I really feared for my life. The image of Emmett Till, a young black boy who was murdered by some angry white men in Mississippi, and his badly mutilated body, which was vividly displayed in a recent edition of Jet Magazine, flashed through my mind.

"Where you live, boy?" he yelled again.

"71 Kracke Street," I whispered.

"I'm gonna take yo ass to jail, boy!" he yelled again.

I believed him, too, as we were heading in the direction of the police station and away from my house.

We rode around for what seemed like hours, but it was really only a few minutes. Eventually, he took me home. Kracke Street never looked so warm and friendly. Mama always waited on the porch for me to come home from school. Today, she sensed that something was wrong as I was a little late. Her fears were confirmed when the huge black car pulled up in front of our house with me inside and a big, white man driving.

He yelled at me to get out and pulled me by my arm through the front gate to our yard. My mother had moved to the top of the stairs. I broke away from the huge policeman's grip and jumped into my mother's arms crying. I tried to get inside her for refuge. I never wanted her to let me go.

"What's wrong?" my mother asked.

"Annie, you better teach that boy of yours some manners," he yelled.

"What did he do?"

"He pushed a white boy into the street and he almost got hit by a car!" he exclaimed.

"Frank!" my mother yelled disappointedly.

"It was Arthur, Momma," I explained.

"Oh, I understand. I'll take care of it, officer."

"You better, Annie," he growled. "The next time I'm gonna take his ass to jail and y'all gonna be in a heap of trouble. You hear me, Annie?"

Mama nodded.

He gave us a mean look of deep hatred that reminded me of the picture of the faces of men who had killed Till. He cut his eyes and sped off in a cloud of dust, leaving the gate open behind him. His car pulled off hurriedly, hurling sand and tiny rocks everywhere. It was a bad experience, but at least he recognized that I was black. I wished that my own people would also see me that way and would quit calling me those terrible names. Sometimes pain also heals I guess. I continued to cling to Mama and was still shaking when she took me inside.

CHAPTER 11

The incident with the policeman reminded me of another hot night in August. We didn't have air conditioning—most people didn't—and the one fan that we owned offered little comfort from the sweltering heat that usually engulfed the Port City. Sweat poured from us in various sized beads. Then, Daddy came up with a great idea. He offered to take us all out for ice cream. There was a great deal of excitement. This was not something that we did very often. I guess that was what made it so special. We began to talk about what flavor we would each get.

My parents, my older brother, Buck, my younger brother, Bobby, and I all got in the car—a 1952 Dodge that my father had purchased used from an old, white lady. This was gonna be a good trip! We each ordered double scoops, which sold for ten cents. For just fifty cents we each had a double scoop of our favorite flavor.

We rode around for a few minutes and then my father pulled over and parked in front of a department store on King Street, which ran through the heart of the downtown area so we could watch some television through the store's front glass. Some stores left the televisions on after they closed. We didn't have a television and it was not unusual for several black people to be crowded around a storefront watching television. In fact, I saw Jersey Joe Walcott lose his heavyweight title to Rocky Marciano through a storefront.

I don't remember what was on television that night, but I do know that the ice cream was good and each of us seemed to be eating it slowly so that the ice cream and the evening would last even that much longer. We had each just about finished our top scoop when this young, white policeman approached our car.

He leaned over, glaring at my father, and asked,

"What are y'all doin' here, boy?"

"We are just eating some ice cream," my father replied.

"Well, y'all can't eat no ice cream round here! You hear, boy?" he yelled. My father had to be at least twice as old as the cop.

You could always tell when my father was about to get upset and possibly lose it, as his top lip would begin to twitch visibly. Mama noticed it and reached over and grabbed my father's hand and whispered, "It ain't worth it, Bill. Please."

"I want you to move this car off the main street and pull over on a side street if you want to eat y'all ice cream, boy!"

My father was trying to remain calm, but I could imagine how he must have felt being ridiculed and made to feel less that a man in front of his family, especially his sons. This was not an uncommon experience for a black man to have to endure for most of his life if he wanted to stay alive and out of jail—and to be there for his family.

"Move on now, boy. Ya hear me or what?" the policeman yelled as he began to unhook his holster.

"Come on, Bill, let's go," urged my mother, rubbing his arm.

Daddy started up the car and pulled away. Momma reached over and squeezed his hand and whispered, "It's all right Bill."

Daddy threw his ice cream out of the window as he rounded a corner and drove straight home. No one said a word or uttered a sound. My ice cream didn't taste good anymore and I just let it drip down my hand until we got home and then I threw it away. Daddy never said a word. He went straight to bed as sleep was his only temporary escape from a reality that would be just as real when the sun rose the next morning. He didn't blow on our stomachs the next morning as he usually did as he tried to quietly leave to go to work, but we heard him anyway. I guess he didn't want to face his boys. I guess, in his mind, how could he?

CHAPTER 12

At ICS we had to say the rosary each day and were required to go to Mass at the Catholic Church around the corner each Friday. Everyone was required to go to mass, but the Protestants were not allowed to participate in the mass. All of the Catholics could dip their hands in the holy water at the entrance to the church, but the Protestants were not allowed to. We were told that if we attempted to do so, our hand would burn off.

My family attended Emanuel A.M.E. Church and we were used to fireball preaching and choirs singing with spirit. The Catholic Church service was conducted in Latin and it was very solemn and quiet and extremely boring. And, there was too much kneeling.

We did alright at ICS despite being ostracized by most of the Catholics and most of the nuns. My older brother, Buck, was at the top of his class and so was my younger brother, Bobby. Bobby was also a National Merit Scholar! I was in the top 5 in my class. I was not as serious a student as Buck and Bobby were or maybe I wasn't as smart.

My brother Buck was also one of the best athletes in Charleston. He excelled at baseball and football. During his junior year at ICS he was voted Most Valuable Player and Best Running Back. He was also one of the smartest kids in Charleston, and was destined to graduate Valedictorian. I was now in the ninth grade and was just trying out for the football team for the first time. The summer after Buck's junior year at ICS something happened that would change our lives forever.

My family and I had just returned from Atlantic Beach, a black beach a few miles from Myrtle Beach. Blacks were not allowed at Myrtle Beach. The ride home took us about an hour and a half. It was around ten o'clock when we got home. We had just unpacked everything from the car and were heating up some water to take our baths to wash off all of the salt water and sand.

About fifteen minutes after we got home the doorbell rang. It was one of our friends. He wanted to know if we could hang out on the corner for a while. That was one of our rituals. About five or six of us would hang out on the corner in front of the Dart's Hall Library. It was only about two doors from our house. Sometimes we could hang out as long as we were within shouting distance of our mother.

Buck decided that he would hang out for a while, and would take his bath later, but I was too tired and decided to stay home. I went into the kitchen and ran some water in a large pot to heat up for my bath. About 45 minutes later the doorbell rang again. It was two black detectives, Mr. Temple and Mr. Wong. My mother could sense that something was wrong when she answered the doorbell and saw them, especially the detectives.

"Hello, Mrs. Godfrey," Mr. Temple uttered with his deep voice.

"Hello, Mr. Temple," my mom almost whispered.

"I'm afraid that I have some bad news for you, Mrs. Godfrey."

"What is it Mr. Temple? Something wrong with my boy?"

"We just arrested Buck."

"You arrested Buck? What for?"

"Murder, Mrs. Godfrey. Murder. A cop just got killed on the corner and Buck is a suspect."

As soon as my mother heard this hives began break out all over her body like popcorn popping under the foil in a bag of Easy Pop Popcorn, and her knees buckled. She had to brace herself against a chair to keep from falling. I had never seen anything like that happen before and have never seen anything like it since. About this time, my father entered the room and held my mother close to him, gently rubbing her back.

"There must be some mistake," my father muttered.

"There is no mistake. I'm not saying that Buck pulled the trigger, but the cop is dead and we arrested everyone who was on the corner. So far, no one confessed so we have to keep all of them. We gotta go now. I'll let you know something as soon as I find out."

"So, where is Billy?" Mama asked.

"They will all be booked and taken to the city jail under the bridge."

One of the city's jails was under the Cooper River Bridge about fifty yards out in the water on the Charleston side. You could see the jail as soon as you approached Charleston from Mount Pleasant. I would always notice that jail, but I never dreamed any one of us would be inside it.

All kinds of thoughts began to run through my mind. I could picture Buck pulling the trigger, although I knew that he didn't own a gun. In fact, I did not know any of our friends who owned a gun.

Buck and some of our friends were sitting on the little stoop in front of the library when this little black boy came running down Kracke Street from Spring Street, headed towards Bogard Street screaming.

"Please help me. Dees white men gonna kill me. Please help me," the boy screamed.

Two white men, running as fast as they could, were right behind the boy, in hot pursuit, yelling for him to stop. The only whites we ever saw in our neighborhood were the milkman, the mailman, and the insurance man. When Buck and our friends saw these two white men chasing the little black boy, they began to chase the white men, thinking that they were saving the boy's life.

During the chase someone pulled a gun and fired one shot. The white cops made it to their car and the one who had been shot slumped over in the seat and died. Only one person knew who had fired the fatal shot and for now he wasn't talking.

News of the killing of a white cop by six black youth spread like a wildfire throughout the city. It would not be safe for any black person to break the law or even be on the street, especially at night.

For two long weeks we sat waiting, hoping, and praying that Buck had not pulled the trigger. That was two of the worst weeks my family and I have ever experienced. Mama paced and Daddy bit on his thumb. We didn't talk about it much, but it was always on our minds.

Finally, someone confessed. His name was James Dayson. He also went to ICS and was a pretty good football player. To be honest, I never believed that Dayson had done it. He was always trying to fit in and get a reputation for being bad, and this confession would let everyone know that he was. He was tried and convicted of murder and surprisingly, did not get the death penalty, but everyone in Charleston knew what the penalty was for killing any white person, especially a cop. Dayson was in prison for about three months when word hit the street that he had died under suspicious circumstances. The court did not give him a death sentence, but he got one anyway. Everyone believed that the prison guards had killed him.

News about the cop's murder was pasted across the front page of the local newspaper every day and could be heard and seen on the local radio and television stations. Many people began to act differently towards us. Then, the news came: my brother Buck would not be allowed to return to ICS although he was not found guilty of any crime. I guess they had finally found a way to get us Protestants out of their Catholic school.

They would allow me and my other brothers to return, but not my brother Buck. My mother met with the principal, a nun named Sister Mary Francis, but the decision had already been made by the white priest who headed the convent. Sister Mary Francis, was one of the meanest nuns at the school. My mother decided that if Buck couldn't go back then none of us would. We transferred to the public schools. Buck and I would go to Burke High School and Bobby would go to Rhett Elementary. It would have been in my tenth year had I returned to ICS.

Buck found out that many of his so-called friends were not really his friends after all, as they did not give him the moral or emotional support he needed and expected. In fact, many of them turned their backs on him completely and began to avoid him like he had the plague.

I also lost contact with many of my so-called friends, except a few who were Protestants. Most of my friends from my neighborhood attended Burke

High School, so I thought that things might not be so bad. Little did I know that transferring to Burke would be so difficult for us. I perceived myself as being seen as the light-skinned Negro who had thought that he was too good to go to the public school and now had no other choice. The next three years would be bittersweet.

Burke was a large school. 385 graduated in my class. It was a sprawling campus, with each building dedicated to a discipline. There was the Science Building, the Art Building, etc. Assignments to homerooms were based on academic promise. Students in homeroom 10-1 for example, had the highest averages or academic promise. I was assigned to homeroom 10-6, although at ICS I ranked number five in my class. On the other hand, it seemed like most of the students at Burke were smart and focused.

Although Buck and I were still going to the same school, we never walked to school together. He always left before I did. I always walked with my friend, Jerry. I assumed that Buck just didn't want to walk to school with his little brother. On the other hand, maybe he didn't want anyone to know that I was his brother. It bothered me, but I never questioned it and never mentioned it to him.

Most of the students at Burke seemed to accept me. I made several friends. I also signed up for the Electronics Shop. We would attend normal classes in the morning and spend the afternoon in "shop." Mr.

Perry was in charge of the shop class. That would be my refuge—I was in shop even when we didn't have class. That was where I "hid out." I was at Burke for three years and never ate in the cafeteria! And most of the time the food smelled good coming from the cafeteria, which was located right next to the building where I took shop. I felt like I wouldn't be welcomed there. Some of us would sneak off campus and buy doughnuts and milk for our lunch. I ate a good breakfast and went home to a good snack before dinner.

I never had any girlfriends at ICS and the same would be true for Burke High. Some of the girls seemed to like me, but I was either too shy or intimidated by them. I liked some of the girls, but saw no reason why they should like me. I did meet this girl that I really liked and she seemed to like me, too. Once I asked her if I could come to her house and visit her and she told me that she would like that, but I could get shot because the boys in her neighborhood didn't like light-skinned people. That hurt. I never asked her if I could come and see her again.

Since I didn't have any girlfriends or didn't seem interested in having any, I was given the name, "woman hater," which was later shortened to "hater." I didn't like it, but it was better than cracker boy!

Although Buck was the top football player at ICS, he was made into a defensive back and seldom got a chance to show his running skills. He was still one of the best players, though. He got a scholarship to

Delaware State and the day Momma and Daddy took him to school was one of the saddest days of my life. I didn't go with them, because I was trying to make Burke's football team.

Jerry and I tried out for the football team, but we were not given any equipment to practice in. We kept going to practice anyway. I didn't want to miss any practices and risk being told not to come to practice anymore. I liked playing football and really wanted to make the team.

Buck and I were good punters, so I decided that I might be able to finally make the team as a punter. I could kick for 40 yards with ease and could easily out kick the punters on the team. One day I was booming kicks and I heard two of the coaches talking.

"Who is that kicking the hell out of that ball?"

"He is the red nigger that transferred from ICS. Fuck him," one of the coaches yelled.

"He can kick, though," the other coach replied.

I continued to come to practice and just before Homecoming, all of the boys who had still been coming to practice were given equipment to scrimmage against the first string team. I was put at nose guard. I weighed every bit of 150 pounds and was placed in front of guys who weighed well over 200 pounds. I had always believed that it was the size of the fight in the dog that mattered more than the size of the dog in the fight and I was determined to hang in there. I made several crushing tackles and showed up some of the starters. I stayed low and drove hard and was constantly in the backfield. I made fourteen tackles!

"Who is that little red nigger?" I heard the head coach ask.

"That's Godfrey, the little red nigger from ICS! You know, the one who can punt," the other coach replied.

"Shit, give that boy a uniform."

Right after practice, I was given some equipment. I had never felt so proud. Now, I had to concentrate on a position. I decided that I would try out for center. Burke had three centers. The smallest was 190 pounds and the other two were about 210-220 pounds. After two weeks of practice, I was the starting center. The other centers were converted to other line positions and one was made into a running back! I was finally feeling accepted and a part of Burke. My training in Kracke Court was paying off. I asked the coach to let me try out for linebacker, but he said that I was too small. I would ultimately play linebacker in college, however, at 170 pounds soaking wet!

The first practice after I got some equipment we had a drill called the "pit." Each player had to stand in the middle of this 10-foot wide circle, which was outlined with lime. The entire team lined up just out-side the circle and when the coach blew his whistle, the first player on the line would spring forward and could use any means at his disposal to drive, push, hit or otherwise force the person out of the circle.

If the first player failed to force you out of the circle, you were given a chance to re-position yourself, the whistle blew again, and the next player would come forcefully toward you. Most of the players were forced out of the circle, but not me.

I withstood the force of the more than forty players and held my ground. I could tell that some of them did not like the fact that they couldn't move me, but I had grown up on Kracke Court, and I was Buck's brother. The largest guy on the team whose nickname was "Big Daddy"—named after Gene Big Daddy Lipscomb of the Baltimore Colts, one of the first really big men in professional football, couldn't move me either. After the exercise many of the stars on the team came up to me and patted me on the back and told me how tough I was. That made me feel real good. I was beginning to feel a part of something.

The next year, a new head coach came in from Maryland State University and immediately gave me the nickname, "whitefolks." That was my playing name the whole time at Burke. It didn't bother me that much. Cracker boy did, though. There was another light-skinned guy who played and his nickname was Whitefolks, Number Two. At least I wasn't being singled out. Anyway, now people were looking beyond my skin color and focusing on my playing ability. That spring, I would also make the baseball team.

During my senior year, our football team was picked to win the state championship. However, the city was also opening a new school on the other side of town, C.A. Brown. Right after our first game, where we had beaten perennial power and favored Booker T. Washington High School out of Columbia, 12-0, half of the team had to transfer to C.A. Brown across town and were not allowed to play for Burke. That killed any chance we had. Before the move, we were an excellent team; after the move, we were just a good team. We did play for the State Championship in baseball though, losing 3-0. I lettered in football and baseball, but never attended an athletic banquet. I was on the teams, but never really felt like I was a part of the teams.

I graduated in May of 1963, finishing 5th out of 385 students. My brother Buck had the highest average in his class but was not allowed to graduate Valedictorian as he hadn't been at the school "long enough." My brother, Bobby, would also graduate at the top of his class. So, 5th was good, but not as good as Buck and Bobby.

The next three months would be some of the most interesting and life-changing times in my life. Dr. Martin Luther King was on the scene and the Civil Rights Movement was in full swing. My brother Bobby was already very active in the movement and I wanted to be involved, too. I will never forget when my parents were called into the Child Welfare Office where one of the officers threatened to take Bobby away from my parents, because they thought that by allowing him to participate in the movement, they were "contribut-ing to the delinquency of a minor." I had never seen my parents so upset and that motivated me even more to want to join the movement.

CHAPTER 13

The Civil Rights Movement was in full swing in Charleston, South Carolina in 1963, as well as in just about every city in America. I was very active in the movement just like my brother Bobby. Initially, Buck chose not to participate. I guess that the close call he had with the cop's murder made him nervous.

Bobby and I would get up early each morning and would be at Emanuel AME Church by 9:00. Emanuel was one of the sites that Harriet Tubman used for her underground railroad to transport escaped slaves from the slavery in the south to freedom in the north.

It was fitting that some of the descendants of the same slaves who used this church as a vehicle to secure their freedom, were now using this church as a vehicle to secure basic human rights allegedly guaranteed to every American under the Constitution. It reminds me of what an ex-slave once wrote, "Slavery and freedom, de is mos de same. Ain't nothing difent sep in de name."

About 200 of us, who were mostly around 18 years old or younger, would meet at Emanuel each morning. We would be fed a light breakfast, which was usually pastries furnished by Mr. Taylor's Bakery, and some juice. We were given our instructions for the morning, which usually consisted of picketing in front of stores with "white" and "colored" signs displayed in the stores, as well as stores that did not hire blacks, which was most stores.

We would also try to discourage the blacks who seemed to not be concerned with discrimination from shopping in these stores. In spite of our demonstrations, you could always find several blacks patronizing the white businesses downtown anyway. Some of them would even want to fight us because we were trying to "tell" them how to spend their money.

I remember how Mama would always carry one of those little plastic cups, which sort of expanded like an accordion in her pocketbook. Blacks couldn't drink at the "white-only" water fountain, which was always clean and had nice ice-cold water all the time. The "colored-only" fountain, which was just tap water, seemed to always have at least one cigarette butt in it, and a huge, dead cockroach could usually be found along with several pieces of chewed gum. I always suspected that some white people had spit their gum in the "colored" water fountain just for spite, before they drank from "their" water fountain.

Anyway, Mama would always look around to make sure that no white folks were looking and she would whip out that little accordion-like cup and would get us some water from the clean, cold "white-only" fountain.

I also remember being hungry many times when we were out shopping with Mama, and she would tell us that we would have to wait until we got home to get something to eat because they didn't serve "us" at the snack bars in the stores. I never could quite understand that.

I also could never understand why we had to sit behind the line when we rode on the city bus. I will never forget the sign that was so conspicuously displayed on every bus in Charleston: "All colored passengers must sit behind the white line." There would be seats in the white section of the bus and many times I would see older blacks standing up behind that line as the bus rolled toward its destination. But Rosa Parks refused to one day!

Anyway, we would march and picket until noon and then it was back to Emanuel for a brief rest from the hot, Charleston sun. We then had some lunch, got our instructions for the afternoon, and would march and picket until 5:00 p.m. After going home for dinner it was back to Emanuel to get the plans for the evening.

We always knew that some of us might be going to jail that night, and some of us might even be hurt or maybe even killed. We accepted these things as a fair price for freedom I guess, or maybe we were just young and crazy!

Since it was usually anticipated that we would be arrested, we were asked to go home, bathe, dress appropriately and bring our toothbrush and a washcloth. Each time we attempted to integrate a restaurant or movie theater, we were dressed like we were going to church—suit or sport coat, shirt and tie.

I arrived home one evening, took a bath, ate, and got my toothbrush, washcloth, and some toothpaste. My mother knew that I was very active in the movement, and although she approved of what we were doing, she felt like most parents, I imagine, worried that something might happen when I went out to demonstrate. Emmett Till's body was deeply etched in the minds of all blacks. I could see the look of worry behind her proud face.

"Where you goin', boy?" she inquired.

"Might go to jail tonight, Mama," I replied.

"What y'all gonna do now, son?"

"Might try and eat at the Fort Sumter Hotel, Mama."

"Boy, y'all crazy?"

"No, ma'am."

My father and older brother were in the room as Mama and I talked. My older brother, Buck, just shook his head and looked at me like I was crazy because I might go to jail. My father, who never had much to say, still said nothing as he read the evening paper and bit on his thumb, which seemed to be his way of dealing with most things.

They were all somewhat active in the movement, but my younger brother Bobby and I were the most active. Mama didn't like the thought of my going to jail, but she knew what we were trying to accomplish, so she didn't interfere. She gave me a big hug and wished me good luck. My father continued to bite on his thumb and Buck continued to shake his head.

We met back at the church. On this particular night, we were divided into several groups of about four or five. Some were to attempt to gain entrance into the "white-only" entrance at several of the local theaters, and the group, which I was assigned to, would attempt to be served at the restaurant at the Fort Sumter Hotel located on The Battery, an exclusive, all-white neighborhood facing the Ashley River.

I remember how the white folks could always go in the movie theater through the front door. It was air-conditioned downstairs where they sat, and they had nice, soft, cushioned seats. They had a nice concession stand and nice, clean restrooms. We had to sit in the balcony, which could only hold about 100 people at a time.

I remember having to wait outside of the movie theater with the other children for several hours until those blacks who were already in the movie had finished watching so we could go in. The white folks could come and go as they pleased during the movie. We had to stand in a long line and wait until we were told that we could go in. You had to wait until the movie was over before you could go in.

The "colored" section was hot and the seats were hard. There was only one toilet and everyone (boys and girls) had to use it. There was no concession stand, but we could buy popcorn and drinks, which were passed to us through a little window at the top of the stairs.

Anyway, there was little else for blacks to do in Charleston so we would wait. Sometimes, we would arrive at around noon and not get out of the movie until six o'clock, because we'd had to wait through at least one and sometimes two showings.

Our group was driven to the Fort Sumter Hotel/ Restaurant about 7:00 p.m. It is a bit ironic that the restaurant was across the river from, and named for, Fort Sumter, where the first shots for freedom were allegedly fired during the Civil War.

The local police were always notified of our plans—for protection, they said. The police were already there with a paddy wagon (a vehicle that re-sembled a van and could transport several persons) when we arrived. We knew that this meant that we would probably be arrested.

As we entered the restaurant, we were met by a very nervous, short, frail white man who was visibly uncomfortable with our presence. He reminded me a lot of the character played by Don Knotts on the Steve Allen Show.

"Can I help you?" he nervously uttered.

"We would like to have dinner," I replied.

"We……..don't…….serve nig……..gers here," he stuttered.

"We don't want to eat any niggers either. We want to eat dinner," my friend, Jerry, retorted.

He became even more nervous.

"You are trespassing on private property and I am asking you to leave," he replied.

We remained silent—just staring him right in his cowardly looking eyes.

"You are trespassing, and I want you to leave these premises immediately," he yelled.

We still remained silent. He went outside and summoned the policemen.

"I have told these niggers that they are trespassing and they still refuse to leave the premises." He yelled this with confidence, now that he had the police officers there with him.

"Would you ask them to leave again, please," said the policeman.

"You are trespassing, and I am asking you to leave these premises," the frightened, little man yelled again.

We still remained silent.

"You are all under arrest," yelled the policeman.

We were led quietly into the waiting paddy wagon and taken to the city police department.

"Got another load of uppity niggers," yelled a policeman as they unloaded us like a herd of animals from the paddy wagon.

We were fingerprinted and had our pictures taken. We were then herded like cattle onto a bus with iron barred windows that was used to transport prisoners. We were taken to the state correctional facility where we would spend four nights and three days before we would see our families again. They claimed that they had to put us in the state facility because all of the other jails were crowded.

We were forced to sleep on the floors just outside of the main cellblock on filthy mattresses, which had a strong smell of urine. We were not given any pillows or sheets. We were placed among the rapists, murderers and thieves. The smell of feces and urine permeated the cellblock.

A guy whom they nicknamed the "undertaker" was in our section. He was doing five years for killing a close friend of mine in cold blood. He had pumped six bullets into my friend's chest. That was the third murder he had committed over the past five years and this was his longest sentence. In those days, you got more time for stealing than for killing a "nigger."

We were warned not to take any showers. We felt that we knew why we were warned, but any doubts we may have had were put to rest when we heard an inmate being raped by another inmate later on that night when the lights in the cell block were turned off.

I had heard that this went on, but it was really difficult for me to just lie there and hear the inmate begging the other inmate not to take advantage of him. His moans and groans could be heard for several minutes until the aggressor was satisfied.

No one bothered us, though. We were special. One of the trustees, a guy named Black, who had a reputation of being one of the toughest guys on the streets of Charleston, warned the other prisoners not to bother us. He told them that, "they are fighting for our freedom."

Although we did not have to go out on the work details with the other prisoners, we did have to eat with them. I remember trying to eat one meal, a breakfast which consisted of so-called corn bread, which tasted like it had been soaked in the water from a rice pot that had been soaking for several hours waiting on someone to wash it out, and two slices of slab bacon that were too hard to bite, much less chew. The only water available was from an old wooden keg with about a half-inch of scum floating on the top of the water. There was also a large, dead cockroach floating on top of the water.

There was a rumor that someone was bringing us some fried chicken dinners, but we never saw them. Someone said that they were intercepted by the guards who ate them. We basically went without food or water for the entire time we were there. There were no windows so we also did not see the sun.

As soon as we got out of jail, we were back on the streets: marching, picketing and singing. There was also a ritual for all recently released Freedom Fighters.

We would all be welcomed back into the fold at the church and would walk down the aisles to a standing ovation. Each person's name would be called along with where he or she had been arrested and for how long. That was a good feeling.

The Fort Sumter Hotel would eventually close and be converted to condominiums. We had our ten-year high school class reunion at the Fort Sumter Hotel in 1973. I was the only one there who remembered that night in 1963 and the days and nights that followed. For some reason, I didn't really enjoy myself.

Not long after this incident, six other boys and I would attempt to swim at Folly Beach, an all-white beach about 20 minutes from our house, located just beyond James Island across the Ashley River Bridge.

When I came home the night before we planned to go to Folly Beach, I began to tell the family and Buck decided to go with me. I guess that he knew that this would be one of the most dangerous things I had attempted to do. He always seemed to feel that he had to protect me, although he had done some things to me that made me feel like he hated me instead of loved me. Maybe he loved me, and at the same time, hated my light skin.

For example, once, we were playing cowboys and Indians, and were using this old, abandoned car as a stagecoach. We had lifted a huge cinder block on top of the car to serve as a strong box. Some of my friends and I were running around the car yelling like the Indians did in the movies and Buck timed it perfectly and pushed the cinder block right on top of my head. I thought that I was going to die. It felt like my head had been split into pieces and I held it tightly with both of my hands and ran to my mother. She hugged me and placed a cold towel on my head and eventually the pain went away. She gave Buck a spanking. I don't know if that really helped, though.

Once Buck threw a huge rock at me and it hit me just below my left ear, leaving a deep gash. That scar is still there today. On another occasion, he held me tightly from behind, while my younger brother, Bobby, hit me on the top of my head as hard as he could with a sixteen ounce Pepsi bottle. I still have that scar, too. Buck hurt me physically and mentally, but he still seemed to care for me.

Anyway, we were going to integrate Folly Beach! While most people saw Dr. King as their leader, mine was a young, twenty-four-year-old Baptist minister from Morris Street Baptist Church—the Reverend James Blake. He had the oratory skills of King, but he was close to our age.

One of the local funeral homes, Fieldings, had provided one of its limos to transport us to the beach. Again, the police were notified. We left Mother Emanuel around noon and headed towards Folly Road, which led directly to the beach. As we rode down Folly Road, we could see a Highway Patrol Car about every mile along the way. Each time we approached one of the patrol cars, one of the officers would get on his two-way radio, apparently announcing our approach.

Finally, we were there. The limo pulled up as close to beach front as it could and the eight of us, none older than nineteen, got out, already in our bathing suits, and headed straight for the water. The whites at the beach looked at us in stunned amazement. There were several police officers there, too. A huge, angry crowd began to form trying to block our entrance to the water when one of the cops yelled for them to move out of the way.

We entered the water and after about ten minutes, the whites began to surround us in the water. We were between them and the Atlantic Ocean. To be honest, I was frightened. It seemed like there were hundreds of them. As they began to move closer towards us yelling obscenities and calling us all kinds of names, one of the cops yelled through a bull horn and told them to let us out of the water.

I will never forget how that angry, white mob divided just wide enough to let us out of the water. It reminded me of the parting of the Red Sea in the Bible. Now, we had to walk back to the pickup point where we had been dropped off.

"Niggers!" they yelled.

"They got a cracker boy with them," one of them yelled, obviously referring to me.

I still wasn't black it seemed.

As we approached the pickup point, I could see

Reverend Blake walking up a slight hill toward us. I imagined it must have felt like Moses coming to rescue the Israelites from Pharaoh. That was a good feeling. We got in the car and headed back to Emanuel. We had done it, but I was shaking in my skin. Was it from the air conditioning in the car on my still-damp body or was I really still afraid?

When we got back to the church, we were treated like heroes for our obvious bravery. One of the boys told about how one of the whites at the beach had referred to me as a cracker boy. One of the leaders mentioned that it is always good to have someone involved that they can't tell whether they are black or not. He suggested that that was a good thing. I didn't see it that way.

Near the end of the summer of 1963, the local leadership in the movement organized a mass march to the office of the local newspaper, The Charleston Evening Post and The News and Courier, to protest its biased and slanted coverage of the protests. The newspapers always made it look like we were under the influence of outside forces, and had communist ties.

About 200 of us gathered at one of the local churches for a brief service and to receive instructions for the march. Non-violence was always stressed with each protest. We were following the example of Dr. King's non-violent movement. We were given the route and would walk four abreast to our destination.

A leader was assigned to every group of twenty marchers to ensure order and that we adhered to non-violence.

When we arrived we were surprised to see many of the national news networks present with their cameras positioned on the top of some of the same buses that were used to transport us to the state correctional facility just weeks earlier. There was also a large number of local and state police present, equipped with riot gear. At least three fire trucks were also positioned nearby. We were confused. Why were the buses, numerous policemen and firemen there? Why was such a peaceful and relatively small demonstration worthy of national coverage? Our questions would be quickly answered!

Shortly after we arrived the police began to attack all of the leaders with billy clubs and drag them off, forcing them into the ready buses. Within a few minutes, you had a group of about 200 individuals without leadership and deeply angered by the police tactics. Someone in the crowd threw a brick at one of the cops who immediately picked it up and hurled it forcefully into the crowd. The huge brick hit a young girl who could not have been more than 12 years old on the side of her leg. The brick broke her leg and one of her bones protruded through her flesh and blood gushed out. The peaceful marchers rapidly evolved into a mob hell-bent on vengeance. A non-violent, peaceful protest turned into a riot that would last for hours.

My mind had never been in such a state. I had always been shy and gentle, but now I had the urge to harm other humans—the white policemen and firemen who were now a real threat to my survival. The cops were beating some of us—men, women and children—and the firemen were using their hoses on us. Everyone was running around and screaming like they were crazy and no one was in charge—no one!

Buck and I were arrested along with several others and placed in one of the buses. When the bus was full it headed to the police station, but about one block from the station, one of the protesters kicked out the back door and we all escaped and returned to the riot.

Surprisingly, no one was killed, but many were seriously injured—protesters, policemen, firemen and innocent bystanders. I alone was responsible for hitting several policemen and firemen with rocks. I used my baseball skills and hit them hard. I never felt good about that, but at the time it seemed like what I had to do. We were under siege and vengeance was mine. It was kill or be killed, or at least that's how it felt.

Eventually, order was restored when some of the leaders were released to help control the crowd, and the local political leaders urged an end to the rioting. We returned to the church. We eventually settled down and were urged to return to our homes. It was now about 2 a.m. We had first met in the church around 7 p.m.

Some angry and armed whites were patrolling the

streets looking for anyone black. We were told to leave in twos and to use "shortcuts" to get home—going through black people's yards and over and under their fences to minimize our presence on the streets. Everyone got home safely. I was exhausted and scared and had already made up my mind that my days of marching and protesting were over. It was almost time for me to go away to college and I didn't like what I had become during the riot, even if only temporarily. "We shall overcome" had become I overcame for me. That was the closest I had ever been to death and the closest I had been to killing someone and I didn't like either feeling. I did go to one more mass meeting, but it was my last. Non-violence is a concept, but even the non-violent can be driven to violence with the right provocation.

CHAPTER 14

The little girl and the brick had sparked a riot, but I suspect that it changed many lives that night, including mine. I would also like to believe that it changed the lives of many of the policemen, firemen and local leaders. Who knows, it may have even changed Charleston.

I never did get a football or baseball scholarship. Buck got both at Delaware State. I did get an academic scholarship at Saint Augustine's College in Raleigh, North Carolina. It is interesting how I wound up there. People had always told me that if I could spend several years in Florida I would get darker. I was determined to go to Florida for just that reason.

When I finished high school, we took a test similar to the SAT, but designed to place black students in black colleges. They had the names of the black schools listed on the test documents and you could send your test scores to any three free of charge. I saw Saint Augustine's and thought that it was in Florida. To say the least, I had mixed feelings when I got a letter of acceptance and a scholarship offer from Saint

Augustine's College in Raleigh, North Carolina! I decided to postpone getting dark and accepted the offer. I also felt that maybe the color of my skin would not matter in Raleigh. Was I in for a surprise!

Saint Augustine's had an excellent football team, but I decided not to try out for the team because I had also decided that since I couldn't go to Florida, I would transfer to Delaware State to play baseball and football with Buck. We had been playing on the same teams since Little League Baseball. I often wondered whether I was really on these teams just because I was Buck's brother. I was a pretty good ball player, but Buck was the best!

I would often watch the football team practice and word finally got around that I was a first string player in high school.

One night, about two weeks before the first game, some of the football players were roaming the halls of Atkinson Hall, the freshman dormitory. They were hazing the freshmen, although some of them were freshmen themselves. Hazing was a ritual at most schools during this period and just about everyone was subjected to it for at least the first two weeks until everyone settled down into their classes.

Four of us were in a friend's room trying to help each other because we were homesick. For most of us, this was our first time away from home. Some of us had also been to summer camp, but most of us, including myself, had never been this far away from home without our families. It was almost like being seasick without the throwing up. It was a new feeling for me and I didn't like it one bit.

One of the guys in the room, Melvin, had been stricken with polio when he was 12, and it had left his right arm completely paralyzed. He had absolutely no control over it. His arm would just sort of hang there, swinging as he moved through the day. In spite of this, Melvin was able to basically function normally, although he did need help with some things like tying his shoes and his tie. His greatest weapon was his strong legs. It seemed that all of the strength from his arm had gone to his legs. He could stand on the side of the top of a desk and could bend all the way down and back up using just one leg!

We could hear the football players moving toward our room, screaming out cuss words at the top of their lungs as they moved from room to room. And, before we knew it, there they were—right in front of us. We braced ourselves for their onslaught. Two of them were freshmen from Miami, Florida.

Like sharks in a frenzy, they pounced on Melvin. One guy took Melvin's bad arm and swung it real hard. Melvin's arm did about two complete revolutions and then it slowly swung like a pendulum until it finally came to rest at his side.

"God dam. This mother fucker is a rubba man. Watch this shit, man!" one of them yelled.

By this time, several other players had entered

the room and they surrounded us. They wanted in on the fun. The guy swung Melvin's arm again and they all bent over in laughter.

I felt sorry for Melvin, but before I knew it, this short, dark-skinned guy, about five-foot eight and weighing no more than 160 pounds, was right in my face.

"Hey, red nigga!" he shouted.

Here we go again, I said to myself. Maybe Raleigh wasn't gonna be any different than Charleston.

"I heard you could play football, nigga." He yelled.

"I played some." I replied.

"Heard you started in high school."

"I did."

"Then why didn't you come out for our team motha fucka?"

I was trying to explain my rationale to him but to no avail.

"You are a lying red bastard. I know why you ain't tryin out."

"Why? I asked.

"Cause you a punk motha fucka. All red niggas are punks. My high school coach told us all about y'all. He said that red niggas ain't shit. And, you ain't shit, red nigga."

"I am sorry that you feel that way," I offered.

"Yeah, motha fucka. Fuck you!!"

My first impulse was to knock him out, but not only were we outnumbered, I couldn't chance being put out of school before I was really in. Besides, I knew that we would probably meet again on some football field as Delaware State played Saint Augustine's. And, if I wound up staying, next year I was determined to wear the blue and white, but even more determined to show this little nigger just who he was fucking with.

So, instead of fighting, I simply went to my room to lick my wounds and hopefully heal. As Brother Bob Marley stated, "He who learns to walk away lives to fight another day." The wounds from my experiences in Charleston were being re-opened and I did not like the feeling. Ignorance was obviously not confined to Charleston. The plantation mentality, which divided many blacks by skin color, was still alive, and unfortunately, is still evident today.

CPSIA information can be obtained
at www.ICGtesting.com
Printed in the USA
LVOW07s0105011217
558258LV00001B/1/P